The Forbidden Script of the Game

The Practical System to Recode the Mind, Inject New Commands, and Reprogram the Life You Live

The Hidden Architecture

Copyright © 2025 The Hidden Architecture
All rights reserved.

ISBN: 979-8-89860-348-9

No part of this publication may be reproduced, stored in a retrieval system, or transmitted in any form or by any means—electronic, mechanical, photocopying, recording, or otherwise—without the prior written permission of the author or publisher. All rights reserved under international and Pan-American copyright conventions.

Legal Notice: This publication is intended for personal use only. You may not modify, distribute, sell, use, quote, or paraphrase any part of this book without explicit consent from the author or publisher.

Disclaimer: The information contained within this book is provided for educational and entertainment purposes only. The author and publisher have made every effort to ensure the accuracy and completeness of the information presented. However, no warranties of any kind are expressed or implied. This book does not constitute legal, financial, medical, or professional advice. Readers should consult qualified professionals before applying any of the information contained herein. By reading this book, the reader agrees that the author and publisher shall not be held liable for any damages, losses, or liabilities caused directly or indirectly by the use or misuse of the information contained in this book, including but not limited to errors, omissions, or inaccuracies.

Before you change the game, you must see it for what it is: a trap disguised as truth.

Table of Contents

Introduction 6

Part I. The Hidden Framework of Control 19

    Chapter 1. The Invisible Game You're Already In 21

    Chapter 2. The Nature of the Script: What Reality Actually Runs On 34

    Chapter 3. The Hijacking: Who Wrote the Script You're Living Now 46

Part II. Disrupting the Code of the Game 58

    Chapter 4. Access Points: Where to Intercept and Rewire the Script .. 60

    Chapter 5. Timeline Drift: Why You're Always in the Wrong Layer of Reality 70

    Chapter 6. Language as Spell: How Words Lock You Into the Game 81

Part III. Accessing the Rewrite Layer 93

    Chapter 7. Stillness as Access: Entering the Rewrite Zone 95

    Chapter 8. The True Mechanics of Manifestation 107

    Chapter 9. The Feedback Loop: How Reality Mirrors the Script in You 117

Part IV. Walking as the Programmer 129

    Chapter 10. Conscious Frequency Control 131

    Chapter 11. Script Collapse and Code Injection 142

    Chapter 12. Exit the Game, Enter the Code 153

Introduction

Why Your Life Feels Scripted

There's a moment, subtle but undeniable, when you begin to sense that something isn't right.

It's not always dramatic. It doesn't require a breakdown or a sudden revelation. Sometimes, it's as quiet as a repeated frustration, a repeated pattern, a repeated emotion that shouldn't make sense anymore. You've grown. You've tried. And still, life circles back like it's following some unseen rhythm.

The job changes, but the feeling returns.

The relationship ends, but the dynamic resurfaces.

The goals shift, but the internal ceiling doesn't move.

It's not coincidence. It's not failure. It's not you.

It's the script.

Most people never realize they're living one. They mistake predictability for stability. They believe repetition means comfort, or that struggle means they simply haven't worked hard enough. But for those who feel the deeper pull, the ones who know that something beneath the surface is operating without consent, the question becomes impossible to ignore:

Why does life feel like it's already been written for me?

The answer doesn't lie in psychology alone. It isn't just trauma, memory, or mindset. Those are only echoes—surface-level consequences of a deeper code that has been quietly installed. A script made of belief systems, energetic loops, emotional frequencies, and thought patterns that were never truly yours to begin with.

You were born into it.

And like most people, you began adapting to survive it before you ever had the chance to question it.

From the moment you were observed, measured, labeled, or rewarded, the script began to embed itself. Not just through language or rules, but through tone, expression, repetition. Through the nervous system. Through moments of shame disguised as learning. Through patterns of approval and punishment disguised as love. This wasn't a personal failing. It was social conditioning so ancient, so embedded, that even those who enforced it didn't know they were obeying something.

The truth is, you've never really been inside the "real world." You've been inside the container of a pattern. A frequency chamber. A looping framework that replicates itself through education, media, relationships, and internalized belief.

And that's why it feels scripted. Because it is.

This isn't a metaphor. The sensation that life is somehow playing out in pre-written cycles is rooted in something real. Something structural. Not supernatural, not conspiratorial, but systemic in a way that most people are trained not to see. You can change cities, partners, habits, and even careers, and still find yourself pulled back into the same psychic and emotional configuration.

The people change.

The setting changes.

But the story doesn't.

This is not your fault. It's also not permanent.

But before you can break it, you have to see how it's built.

The script is not made of words on a page. It is constructed from responses. It's how you interpret silence. It's what you believe you're allowed to want. It's the rhythm of self-doubt that kicks in right when opportunity gets close. It's the way you prepare for rejection without realizing you're doing it. The way you sabotage intimacy or shrink around power. It's the instinct that tells you not to risk too much. The old voice that says, "You know how this ends."

Except… you don't. Not really.

But the script does. And it's been running the scene before you even arrive.

That's the part no one talks about.

The fact that reality, for most people, is preloaded.

Not with fate. Not with destiny.

But with patterns so deeply embedded they become invisible.

Once you understand that, everything changes.

Not because the world around you bends immediately, but because for the first time, you see where the lines have been drawn.

You begin to ask: Who wrote this?

And more importantly: Can I write something else?

That question is where the loop ends.

But to reach that point, we must first pull the curtain back on how the script installs itself.

It begins subtly. Not through overt control, but through emotional repetition. The child praised for being "quiet" learns to dim their fire. The one scolded for asking too many questions learns to obey. Over time, these micro-responses accumulate, carving out a shape in the psyche. That shape becomes identity. But it isn't truly yours. It's a structure you learned to wear. That identity begins to attract specific experiences, people, reactions. It's not mystical—it's pattern logic. Like a magnet tuned to a particular charge, your internal code emits signals that pull matching elements into your field. If your code includes unworthiness, you'll encounter experiences that reflect it. Not because you deserve them, but because the script running your energy doesn't recognize any other outcome.

This is where most people get stuck. They try to change outcomes at the surface. They chase new goals. Repeat affirmations. Change relationships. But the code stays the same. And so, the pattern continues. Until the script itself is interrupted, nothing truly shifts.

This isn't about self-blame. It's about self-awareness. The point is not to shame yourself for running an old program. It's to notice that it *is* a program—and that it can be rewritten. But you can't fight what you can't see. And you can't rewrite what you keep rationalizing.

The most dangerous part of the script is how natural it feels. You don't question it because it wears your voice, mimics your instinct, pretends to be intuition. It becomes the path of least resistance. The expected reaction. The predictable shutdown. And because it's familiar, it becomes "truth."

But familiarity is not truth.

Repetition is not reality.

And identity is not fixed.

Every script you've ever lived was installed. Some were inherited. Others were absorbed. A few were copied. But none were born with you. That means none are sacred. All can be questioned. And all can be broken.

This book is not about spiritual optimism. It isn't interested in whether you feel good about that idea. It's interested in whether you'll see the mechanics and take control. Because control is not manipulation. It's authorship. When you become the author of your experience, reality begins to listen differently.

You'll feel it first in the spaces where you used to shrink. A conversation you'd avoid suddenly becomes neutral. A voice in your head that once sounded final begins to feel mechanical. The old triggers still appear, but you don't collapse into them. Something has shifted. You've stepped out of the scene and into the director's chair.

That shift isn't poetic. It's structural.

And it starts here—by naming the feeling you've been living in for years: *This isn't mine.*

Once you can say that with clarity, not anger, you've reclaimed the first lever of power. You don't need to know how to fix it yet. You don't need a master plan. You only need to see the false as false. Because once that happens, the loop can't hold itself together. It begins to flicker.

You're not here to be managed by beliefs that you didn't choose. You're not here to react to expectations you never set. You're not here to live the echo of a childhood you've outgrown. That's not evolution. That's repetition.

And repetition without awareness is a cage.

You are here to interrupt. To disturb the known. To collapse the familiar if it no longer serves you. That's the energy the system can't handle—because the system thrives on predictability. But when you stop responding the way you were trained to, the whole sequence breaks.

It doesn't take decades.

It takes precision.

A clear decision that the script is not the authority.

You are.

From this point forward, every tool, every concept, and every method in this book is aimed at one thing: handing you the pen.

The story isn't over. But the page is yours now.

The Original Blueprint: What They Erased from Human Memory

Something ancient still lingers beneath the static of modern life.

It hums just below language. It pulses in symbols we no longer understand. It moves through the architecture of old myths, forgotten rituals, and half-remembered instincts. And though most can't name it, every person alive has felt it at some point—the haunting sense that we've lost something. Not just knowledge, but a kind of original orientation. A memory that doesn't exist in the mind, but in the body. In the field. In the code.

You weren't born disconnected.

You were severed.

Not by chance. Not by evolution. But by systems designed to overwrite something older. Systems that told you reality was fixed, linear, and external. That everything you needed was outside of you. That truth could only come through authority. That anything invisible was either irrelevant or dangerous.

But before all of that, there was something else.

There was a blueprint.

The human blueprint wasn't meant to be passive. It wasn't designed to consume information and obey instructions. It was an active interface—a direct link between consciousness and form. You were never supposed to manifest from need, chase outcomes, or manipulate your way into alignment. You were wired to resonate. To emanate frequency that shaped matter. To broadcast identity and attract matching outcomes like magnetic code. Not as a trick. As a biological truth.

Ancient cultures hinted at it, though they used different language. In Egypt, the term *heka* referred to the force that made thought real. In Vedic systems, *tapas* described the inner fire that shaped destiny through attention. In esoteric Christianity, the *Logos* was not a person—it was the creative pattern that spoke reality into being. These weren't metaphors. They were descriptions of a mechanism, a process that linked intention to reality through unseen structure.

That structure was the blueprint.

It mapped the connection between mind, emotion, frequency, and environment. It showed how thought moved into form through coherence.

How a person's inner state literally tuned the world around them. And how disconnection from that pattern led to distortion, fragmentation, and suffering.

But here's what matters most:

That blueprint wasn't mystical. It was practical.

It could be taught. Practiced. Applied.

And that's exactly why it had to be erased.

Not destroyed. Just buried.

Drowned beneath culture.

Rewritten through fear.

Replaced with scripts of control, hierarchy, and dependency.

If people remembered how their reality actually responded to them—directly, and without permission from any institution—they wouldn't need systems. They wouldn't obey. They wouldn't be manageable. Because their power wouldn't come from permission. It would come from clarity. A clarity rooted not in belief, but in design.

That clarity is what this chapter is here to help you begin to remember.

This isn't about nostalgia for ancient times. The point is not to look back, but to reach beneath. The blueprint isn't behind us. It's still there. Under the conditioning. Under the pattern. Under the noise. You don't need to recover it from a lost civilization. You need to unmute it in your own system.

That begins with understanding what was replaced—and why.

The modern human is trained to think in fragmentation. To separate thought from body. Emotion from logic. Energy from matter. But none of these were ever meant to be divided. The blueprint was whole. It functioned through unity, not contrast. It didn't say "you must be positive" or "never feel doubt." It operated like music—allowing for rise and fall, dissonance and return. It allowed for feedback. It adapted without losing its structure.

It wasn't a doctrine. It was a field.

One you're still connected to, even now.

But to access it again, you'll need to dismantle the noise that was placed in its way. The cultural programs, spiritual distortions, and emotional contracts that keep your frequency bound to a lower pattern.

We'll start there. You'll need to dismantle the noise that was placed in its way. The cultural programs, spiritual distortions, and emotional contracts that keep your frequency bound to a lower pattern.

These distortions were not random. They were introduced through repetition. Through systems of education that favored memorization over perception. Through religions that externalized divinity and made power conditional. Through media that trained you to crave stimulation but fear stillness. Through institutions that offered safety in exchange for obedience. Over time, these signals embedded themselves not just in your thinking, but in your nervous system.

What this did was scramble the signal.

Instead of broadcasting the blueprint—your natural frequency—you began to broadcast confusion, contraction, and contradiction. The field around you still responded, but it mirrored back chaos. Not because you were broken, but because your signal was distorted. You were still creating. You never stopped. But without the original pattern as your guide, your creations became unstable, reactive, and loop-based.

This is why many people who study manifestation or energetic work end up feeling frustrated. They are activating fragments of the blueprint without restoring the whole. They visualize while unconsciously holding fear. They affirm what they don't believe. They ask the universe for outcomes they have no energetic alignment with. And then they wonder why it doesn't work. Or worse, why it sometimes does—only to collapse.

The original blueprint never functioned through force. It responded to coherence. Alignment. Wholeness. Not perfection, but resonance. When a person's thoughts, feelings, and energy are speaking the same language, reality has no choice but to organize around them. It is not personal. It is mechanical. The field doesn't respond to words. It responds to structure.

That structure was your birthright. And even if it has been buried, it hasn't been deleted. You've already felt it. In moments of sudden clarity. In the silence after something ends and the truth rises unfiltered. In the instant you stop chasing and begin receiving. These flashes are not anomalies. They are reminders. Traces of the original code resurfacing in real time.

And you don't need to chase them.

You need to stabilize them.

The first step is to stop identifying with the distortion. You are not the noise. You are not the confusion. Those are overlays. Scripts laid across your signal. You don't need to fix yourself. You need to remove what was never you.

The second step is remembering how power actually feels. It doesn't feel loud. It doesn't feel aggressive. It doesn't even feel like effort. True power feels quiet. Anchored. Clean. It doesn't spike. It doesn't need to convince anyone. It moves reality because it is already reality.

That feeling is your compass. Not motivation. Not hype. Not performance. The blueprint recalibrates when you stop chasing and start tuning. And tuning happens when you stop reaching outward for confirmation. Every time you override your internal signal to meet someone else's expectation, you weaken the field. Every time you pretend to be less than you are to avoid judgment, the code fragments. Every time you defer to a system that denies your inner knowing, you tell the blueprint it is irrelevant.

But the moment you reverse that flow—when you begin acting in alignment even when no one else sees it—the field begins to respond. Reality starts to reconfigure. Not instantly, but structurally. Quietly. Permanently.

That is what was erased.

Not your power, but your awareness of it.

And now, you remember.

Not as an idea, but as a design. One that is still running beneath the layers. One that is waiting to be activated again. Not through belief. Through embodiment.

Everything that follows in this book is meant to bring you back into contact with that code. To strip away what was layered over it. To help you recognize the difference between the signal and the noise. Between the script and the truth.

You are not here to learn something new.

You are here to remember what was never allowed to fully activate.

And the moment that memory becomes action, the script loses its grip. Because nothing overrides the original blueprint. Not for long. Not when it begins to pulse again inside the one who carries it.

Are You the Player, the Pawn, or the Programmer?

Most people believe they're making choices. That they're acting with free will, thinking independently, creating outcomes through strategy or effort. But if you look closer, something else becomes visible. The same patterns play out again and again. The same emotional triggers. The same limitations dressed in different circumstances. Despite intelligence or effort, most people are not creating—they are reacting.
There's no shame in that. But it does raise the question:

What position are you actually playing in the Game?

The Game is not metaphorical. It's the energetic and psychological architecture you move through every day. It includes your thoughts, actions, beliefs, environment, and the silent agreements you've inherited without question. And in this structure, everyone is operating from one of three positions—whether they realize it or not.
Each of these positions carries a distinct frequency. A specific relationship to power, reality, and possibility. Understanding which one you're currently operating from is the first step to changing it.
Let's break them down.

The Pawn

The pawn doesn't know there's a Game. They follow the script without questioning its origin. Their decisions are reactive, shaped by rules they didn't create. Their goals are borrowed, their identity shaped by external feedback. They often feel powerless but hide that feeling behind productivity or performance.
The pawn is not unintelligent. Often, they are deeply thoughtful, sensitive, even spiritual. But they are still bound by invisible constraints. They seek validation. They wait for permission. Their sense of reality is externally referenced. They follow systems because they're afraid of collapsing without them.
Key markers of a pawn:
- They justify their limits with logic.

- They often say, "I know what I should do, but I don't do it."
- Their energy fluctuates based on what others think or expect.
- They doubt their intuition when it contradicts authority.
- They believe they are "working toward freedom" but remain in cycles.

The pawn is not broken. But they are still asleep in the system.

The Player

The player knows there's a Game. They understand rules can be bent, outcomes influenced, structures navigated. They are strategic. Focused. They invest in power and outcome. They know how to win, or at least how to keep from losing. They seek leverage and clarity. They play to move forward.

The player has begun to wake up. They are aware of energetic influence. They recognize patterns. They've likely explored tools like manifestation, discipline, or subconscious work. But they still see reality as something to master rather than something to reprogram. They are working within the code—but not yet rewriting it.

Key markers of a player:
- They believe success is earned through conscious control.
- They oscillate between flow and force.
- They have tasted freedom, but it still feels conditional.
- They sometimes sense a deeper level beneath their strategy.
- They are not waiting—but they are still efforting.

The player is powerful. But they are still bound by the board.

And then, there's the third role...

The Programmer.

But before we define it, take a moment.

Not to decide who you want to be, but to honestly assess where you are now.

Close the book for a second and ask:

Am I reacting more than I choose?

Do I wait for things to change, or do I quietly shift the current beneath them?

Do I live from a place of fear disguised as logic?
Do I play to win, or do I choose the rules?
Because where you are is not a judgment.
It's a signal.
And what you do with that signal determines whether you stay there—or move forward.
The Programmer does not play the Game. The Programmer *writes* it.
They are not reacting to life. They are not trying to win within the system. They are not seeking leverage or advantage inside a structure built by others. They are operating from a layer underneath. A layer where perception creates form, and identity generates response.
The Programmer understands something most never do: reality is not fixed. It is recursive. It feeds on your inputs. And those inputs are not just your actions, but your emotional frequency, your mental framework, your unconscious agreements, your hidden expectations. These are the variables that shape what happens next.
Where the pawn looks for direction, and the player looks for mastery, the Programmer returns to source. They ask different questions. They move from a place of stillness, not because they're passive, but because they've stopped chasing. They've remembered that alignment creates momentum. That presence reshapes probability. That reality doesn't need to be forced when you're tuned to the layer beneath cause and effect.
The Programmer is not perfect. They don't have everything figured out. But they are awake, not just to the external Game, but to the architecture behind it. They recognize that thoughts are not tools—they are code. That emotion is not a reaction—it's a signal amplifier. That every belief is a line in a script that either loops or evolves, depending on how it is written.
When something goes wrong, they don't panic. They observe. When they hit resistance, they don't fight harder. They change the script. They don't ask, "Why is this happening to me?" They ask, "What part of me is running this program?" And then they rewrite it. Quietly. Precisely.
This is not metaphor. This is the actual mechanism of transformation.
It doesn't require constant action. It requires consistent alignment. It requires the ability to hold an internal signal without collapsing into the noise. It requires mastery over where your energy goes, what you believe by default, and what you allow to loop without intervention.

You don't have to be a mystic to be a Programmer. You don't need to meditate for hours or abandon your goals. What you need is inner coherence. A clear signal. The ability to catch yourself in the middle of the scene and remember: "I can choose something else."

And from that point forward, you can.

That is what this book is designed to activate. The part of you that already knows how to shift timelines, collapse patterns, redirect energy, and reframe identity. Not through hype. Through code. Through remembering that nothing in your life has ever been random. It has been responding to inputs you were trained to ignore.

Now that you've seen these roles clearly, the work begins.

You are not locked into one identity. You may have been a pawn last year. A player last week. A Programmer only in brief moments. That's fine. The goal is not perfection. The goal is transition. To begin operating more frequently from the level of the script, rather than inside its loops.

Start by observing. Listen to your language. Track your default responses. Feel the energy behind your decisions. Is it reactive, or intentional? Are you choosing from presence, or from habit? These small awareness shifts are not small. They are access points. They are how you step out of the Game and into authorship.

The rest of this book will guide you through that shift. Not just in theory, but in tools. In sequences. In mechanisms.

Because you don't need to play harder. You need to write better.

And now you will.

Part I. The Hidden Framework of Control

You were never meant to question the rules. That's the first rule.

From the beginning, you were taught to adapt, to accept, to participate. Not to observe, and certainly not to disrupt. You were given rewards for compliance, not clarity. Encouraged to succeed within systems you didn't design. And somewhere along the way, you began to believe that this was the only way to live. That control came from effort, from doing it right, from earning your place inside the structure.

But the truth is, you were born into a Game whose architecture was never explained to you.

This Game is not just political, economic, or social. It's energetic. Psychological. Neurological. It doesn't need your belief to function—it only needs your participation. And the more you move through it unconsciously, the more it feeds. Not on your time. On your attention. Your creative force. Your unclaimed potential.

Part I is not about waking you up to the idea that something is off. If you've picked up this book, you already know that. You've felt the loops. You've watched patterns repeat themselves under different names. You've asked the quiet questions that most people never let themselves speak aloud.

This section is about something deeper. It's about showing you how the system *actually runs* beneath the surface. Not through laws or politics, but through scripts. Emotional scripts. Mental scripts. Invisible contracts you didn't sign but still follow.

The truth isn't hidden because it's complex. It's hidden because it's simple—and because you've been trained not to see it. You've been told that your thoughts are your own. That your feelings come from within. That your beliefs are personal. But none of that holds up under close inspection. What you'll find here is that most of what you take as "you" is actually a reflection of the framework you were dropped into.

This is not to disempower you. It's the opposite. Because once you see the mechanics, you are no longer just reacting. You are no longer running on borrowed code. You begin to perceive your own signal beneath the static.

And in that clarity, something changes.

You stop trying to fix yourself and start seeing the script. You stop searching for the next strategy and start sensing the architecture behind your experience. You stop moving from default settings and begin authoring from the root.

That's what this first part initiates.

You will not be asked to agree with everything. You will not be told what to believe. What you will be given is a lens. A way of seeing what has always been there, quietly shaping your choices, looping your desires, and defining the limits of your perception.

Once you see the framework, you cannot unsee it.

And once you begin noticing the code, the real shift begins.

So let's go in.

Not to rebel against the system.

But to rise above it.

Because once you understand how control is installed, you'll understand exactly how to remove it.

Chapter 1. The Invisible Game You're Already In

The Control Grid: How Rules Are Imposed Without Your Consent

Most of the rules you follow were never introduced to you as choices. They were not offered, explained, or negotiated. They were simply absorbed—layer by layer, moment by moment—until they became so familiar you stopped noticing them.

This is how the Control Grid operates.

Not through visible chains, but through the silent enforcement of expectation.

It begins early. Long before language takes shape. You sense what gets rewarded. You feel what gets punished. You notice what parts of yourself are safe to show, and which parts draw discomfort from others. Your nervous system begins to adapt before your conscious mind can even form questions.

And just like that, the internal rewiring begins.

This isn't conspiracy. It's conditioning. And it's universal.

Every culture, every structure, every institution plays a role in reinforcing the Grid. It doesn't need to be evil to be effective. Most of the people passing these codes to you believed in them completely. They were caught in the same system. They handed down the script because it was handed to them.

The Grid is not about control through force. It's about control through normalization. It's about building an invisible frame around your perception, then convincing you there's nothing outside it.

You were told what success looks like.

You were told what to fear.

You were told what's possible and what's irresponsible.

You were told when to speak and when to be quiet.

And even when no one was telling you directly, the signals were still there. In the media you consumed. In the language you learned. In the tension you felt when your truth didn't match your surroundings.

The Grid trains you to doubt what you feel.

To second-guess the part of you that doesn't align with the world. To trust the structure over your own signal.

And that is the deepest layer of control: not fear, not obedience, but internalized distortion. A split between what you know and what you're allowed to act on.

This split becomes identity. You stop acting from what's real and start performing what is safe. Over time, the performance becomes automatic. You forget it was ever a mask. You start calling it "personality." You defend it, even though it doesn't feel alive.

The Grid rewards that defense. It offers comfort for consistency. Predictability. Predictability makes you manageable. And being manageable earns you approval, opportunity, and belonging—at least on the surface.

But underneath, something contracts.

The real you begins to shrink. Not because it's weak, but because it's been told it is dangerous. That to be fully expressed is to risk disruption. That to challenge the rules is to lose connection, safety, or value. So you quiet the questions. You manage the energy. You play the part.

And you tell yourself it's normal.

But something in you knows it's not.

You feel it when you say yes to things you don't believe in.

When you hide the most potent aspects of yourself.

When you shrink to stay inside someone else's comfort zone.

You feel it when life becomes a series of adjustments instead of a source of creation.

That sensation is not anxiety. It's your system trying to wake up.

What most call confusion is often a signal. A signal that the Grid has started to crack. That your alignment with its rules is wearing thin. That the energy it takes to stay inside the program is no longer sustainable.

And that signal matters.

Because once it gets loud enough, everything changes.

You begin to notice what you once dismissed. The tension in your body during a conversation that asks you to betray your intuition. The subtle energy drop when you agree to something out of fear. The emotional weight of decisions that serve survival, not truth. These moments were always there, but now they stand out like static in a song you used to love. They are interruptions in the Grid's signal. Small fractures in the code.

And once you see them, you can't unsee them.

This is not a call to rebel against everything. It's not about dismantling society or isolating yourself from the world. That would still be a reaction—still a movement defined by the Grid. The deeper work is more precise than rejection. It's reclamation. You're not here to destroy the structure. You're here to stop letting it dictate what is real.

When you begin to question the automatic rules, you discover that most of them are illusions of necessity. The idea that productivity equals worth. That failure is shameful. That certainty is safety. That being seen is dangerous. These aren't truths. They are inherited contracts. You didn't write them. But you've been signing them your whole life.

Here is the cost: every time you obey a rule that isn't yours, you reinforce the Grid. You confirm the falsehood that external structure is the source of meaning. You tell your subconscious, "This is how the world works," and it listens. It continues to shape your reality accordingly. You stay inside the loop, not because you believe in it, but because you haven't actively chosen otherwise.

This is why awareness alone is not enough. You can understand the problem and still live inside it. You can see the Grid and still comply. What breaks the loop is action. Quiet action. Subtle action. The kind that no one applauds, but everything responds to. The kind that rewrites your alignment without needing permission.

You say no when you used to perform agreement.

You slow down when urgency was your default survival code.

You create without asking if it will be accepted.

You stop translating your intuition into something palatable.

You stop softening your power to make others feel safe.

These decisions may seem small, but they are not. They are acts of internal sovereignty. Each one removes a thread from the Grid's hold on you. Each one tells your nervous system, "We are no longer obeying distortion." And that message changes everything.

The Grid loses power not when you fight it, but when you no longer feed it. When you no longer leak energy into compliance. When your alignment becomes more important than being understood, more important than being approved, more important than being predictable.

This is the beginning of authorship.

You start to move from a different place. You begin making decisions that are no longer based on scripts, but on signal. You feel the difference between a reaction and a response. Between a conditioned yes and a real one. Between the fear of rejection and the freedom of presence.

From the outside, nothing may look different. But internally, the shift is irreversible. Because once you remember what it feels like to be unbound, you will never again confuse survival with living.

This subchapter isn't just an explanation of control. It's a permission slip to notice where it lives in you. Not as a concept, but as a lived pattern. And to begin making choices—not dramatic ones, not performative ones, but intentional ones—that begin to drain the system of its influence.

That's how the Grid collapses.

Not all at once. Not with noise.

But through quiet refusal.

Through the return of your signal.

And through the recognition that rules only bind those who forget they can choose.

Why You Keep Repeating the Same Loops

There's a moment that haunts you more than failure: the realization that you've been here before.

Different details. Same cycle. Another relationship ends the same way. Another opportunity crumbles at the edge of momentum. Another decision brings you right back to the same emotional ground you swore you'd outgrown.

You wonder if you're cursed, broken, or just unlucky. But what if none of those are true? What if the repetition has nothing to do with morality, and everything to do with mechanics?

Most people don't realize that the human mind is wired to repeat. Not because it's flawed, but because it's efficient. Repetition is the default survival protocol. Once your subconscious learns a pattern—especially one linked to emotional intensity—it stores it as a shortcut. It tells itself, "This worked once. It kept us alive. Let's keep doing it."

The problem is, survival patterns don't care about fulfillment. They don't ask if you're thriving. They only ask, "Are we safe?" If the answer is yes, the pattern stays—even if that safety is toxic, constricting, or false.

Let's say you were raised in an environment where your voice wasn't welcome. Maybe every time you spoke up, it caused tension or got ignored. Your subconscious learned that silence equaled safety. So you grew up and silenced yourself in jobs, relationships, and decisions. It wasn't weakness. It was strategy. But now, that strategy is a cage.

Here's the twist: the more often a loop runs, the less visible it becomes. You stop questioning it. It becomes who you think you are. That's why loops feel like fate. They become identity.

But they're not who you are. They're just unrevised code.

What most people don't do—what you're about to do—is trace that code back to its source. That's how you exit the loop: not by fighting the pattern, but by becoming aware of its design.

Mapping Your Repeating Loop

To make this practical, you need to track the cycle that's running. And not just mentally. It needs to be externalized. Written. Seen. Let's do that now.

Choose a loop. The one that hurts the most. The one you feel when you're alone. The one that makes you say, "Why does this always happen to me?" Now break it down:
- What is the emotional trigger that begins it? (It often starts subtle: a rejection, a comment, a silence.)
- What behavior or reaction do you default to immediately afterward?
- What outcome does this pattern consistently lead to?
- What internal story do you tell yourself to make sense of the outcome?

This sequence—trigger → behavior → outcome → story—is your loop.

Let's say your loop starts when someone questions your abilities. You feel an old shame flare up. You immediately overwork to prove yourself. Eventually you burn out, and when things collapse, you say, "See? I'm not good enough." That story reinforces the shame. The loop closes, ready to restart next time.

The most dangerous part of this cycle is the story. Because the story makes the pattern feel like reality.

Pause here.

You've just mapped one of your deepest unconscious programs. That's not small. Most people never do this their entire life. They just keep running the loop and wondering why nothing changes. But now you're seeing it. Noticing where it starts, how it runs, and what lie it closes with.

That's where your power begins—not in perfection, but in precision.

We'll now move toward the real shift: learning how to interrupt the loop in real time, and eventually rewrite the code behind it.

The moment you can see a loop, it starts to lose control over you. It becomes an object in your awareness rather than something you live inside without questioning. The real transformation begins not with resistance, but with recognition.

Most people try to force themselves out of a loop through willpower. They attempt to override the pattern by sheer effort, but this is why most change feels like a temporary high followed by collapse. Willpower is not a sustainable operating system. Your subconscious runs the show, and it does not respond to pressure. It responds to repetition and emotional precision.

To escape a loop, you must create a disruption strong enough to override the existing pattern. That disruption must feel safer than the original. This is why many people fail to change. They try to replace a familiar pain with an unfamiliar freedom, but the unfamiliar still feels dangerous to the subconscious.

You have to go deeper than tactics. You must become the observer and the editor.

Interrupt and Rewrite

Now that you've mapped your loop, it's time to practice disruption. But not randomly. You need to intercept the loop at the most fragile link. And that's usually the story.

The story is what justifies your loop. It makes the whole cycle seem logical and inevitable. "I always ruin things," "People always leave," "I'm not meant to be successful"—these are not facts. They are conclusions drawn from repeated experiences, written by a part of you trying to make sense of chaos. The story gives your loop meaning, but it also keeps you bound to it.

The simplest, most powerful disruption is to change the internal story. And not through fake affirmations or blind optimism. The goal is not to lie to yourself, but to introduce a new narrative that holds more truth.

Start with questions that dismantle the old logic:
- What if that trigger didn't mean what I thought it meant?
- What if my reaction is not the only possible one?
- What if the outcome was not a reflection of who I am, but of an outdated program running through me?

These questions weaken the authority of the loop. They create space for something new.

Once you've asked them, insert a new sentence. A sentence that feels slightly uncomfortable but not impossible. It might be:

"I am not who I was when this loop was created."

Or:

"Just because I've reacted this way before doesn't mean I have to again."

The loop only continues because you keep agreeing with it. The moment you withdraw that agreement, even slightly, the pattern begins to fracture.

This is the real work. It's not glamorous. It doesn't always feel powerful. But it is the foundation of reprogramming. You are retraining the part of your mind that believes comfort equals truth. You are taking your identity back from patterns that were installed in you without permission.

The more you do this, the faster the loop loses energy. Eventually, the trigger happens and the old reaction doesn't show up. Or it shows up weaker, quieter. You catch it mid-cycle. You choose differently. And it ends. Not because you fought it, but because you outgrew it.

That's how power works. Not in massive declarations, but in subtle shifts that rewire the code underneath your behavior. You do not need to become someone else. You need to become the one who writes the script.

And now, you know how to find the part that keeps getting repeated. You've traced its structure, seen its illusion, and broken the trance.

From this point on, every time the loop tries to restart, you'll see it for what it is: a default setting, not your destiny.

You are no longer looping. You are learning. And soon, you'll be the one designing the pattern.

How the Game is Hidden Behind Logic, Language, and Emotion

You've probably felt it before—an invisible wall you can't name. Something feels off, manipulated, staged. But when you try to explain it, logic kicks in and tells you you're being paranoid. Emotion swells, clouding your clarity. Words suddenly feel too small to describe what you sense.

That's not an accident. It's design.

If someone wanted to keep a population contained, they wouldn't just use chains. They'd program the mind to self-regulate. They'd disguise the walls as "common sense," the chains as "normal feelings," the control system as "language."

Welcome to the invisible architecture of control: logic, language, and emotion.

Each of these forces is neutral in essence. But in the wrong hands, they become tools of distortion. You're not only taught what to think—but how to think, how to feel, how to speak about what you experience. And without realizing it, you start living by a script you didn't write.

Let's break each one apart.

Logic: The Illusion of Objectivity

You've been taught that logic is pure. That it saves you from irrationality. That it leads to truth. But logic isn't truth—it's structure. And it can be used to support a lie just as easily as to support a truth.

The dangerous part is that once something feels logical, your brain stops questioning it. This is how entire systems of belief get installed. It's how control structures hide in plain sight.

Take this example: "If you don't have money, it means you're not working hard enough." That sounds logical. But it ignores structural inequality, generational disadvantage, energy misalignment, and systemic manipulation. Still, the sentence loops like a script in your head, reinforcing shame.

The power of logic is not in its content. It's in its frame.

Who decided what counted as logical? Who taught you that emotional truth was less valid than intellectual argument? Who made you believe that anything outside of rationality was "crazy"?

When the framework is rigged, the logic becomes a trap. And the trap is invisible because it looks like intelligence.

Language: The Hidden Spellbook

Words are symbols. They point to meaning, but they are not the meaning itself. Yet from childhood, you've been taught to treat language as the highest authority. If you can't explain something in words, it's "not real." If someone else defines a term, their definition becomes the rule.

But language is not neutral. Every word carries bias, history, and programming.

Think of how the words "obedient," "logical," "professional," or "crazy" are used. They don't just describe behavior—they assign value, often subconsciously. When someone calls you "emotional," it's not just an observation. It's a control move, especially if used to discredit your perspective.

Control doesn't always need to shout. Sometimes, it whispers through definitions. Sometimes, it hides in the absence of a word. If you don't have the language to describe your experience, you can't communicate it. If you can't communicate it, you can't connect it. If you can't connect it, you stay isolated—and easily controlled.

This is why certain terms are suppressed. Why mystical concepts are ridiculed. Why emotions are translated into "symptoms" and intuition is filed under "woo."

When language is owned, thought becomes leased.

Emotion: The Ultimate Lever

Emotion is the raw energy of human experience. It fuels every decision, belief, and action—even when you think you're being "rational."

But if you don't understand how emotion works, you'll be manipulated by it constantly.

You'll chase validation because it relieves anxiety. You'll shut down your voice because confrontation triggers fear. You'll sabotage abundance because guilt makes success feel dangerous.

When emotion is unexamined, it becomes an entry point for manipulation. Politicians, marketers, influencers, even loved ones—anyone who understands your emotional blueprint can steer your perception without force.

And this is where the real script hides.

The game is not controlled by violence. It's controlled by stimulus and response. By feelings that rise and fall on cue, conditioned into you over years. By the emotional GPS you were never taught to program yourself.

Script Trigger Decoder

If your reality is being shaped by unseen forces embedded in logic, language, and emotion, then the first step to reclaiming it is not to fight them, but to *see* them. Awareness dissolves programming. Precision restores sovereignty. You need to become fluent in the patterns that shape your perception.

The mind runs on triggers. Every time a script activates, there's a spark — a phrase, tone, memory, look, or belief that sets it off. And once triggered, the loop plays automatically unless interrupted.

This is your decoder: tracing the signal back to its origin and editing the default response.

Let's build the tool.

Step 1: Identify the Pattern

Start with the emotion. Think of a recurring moment in your life where your reaction feels *automatic* — like you're watching yourself repeat something you've done before. It could be shutting down in arguments, chasing approval, going quiet in groups, overexplaining, self-sabotaging just before success.

The key is that it feels familiar, repetitive, and slightly out of your control.

Write it down as clearly as you can: "When [X] happens, I usually [Y]."

Now ask: what emotion floods in first? Is it fear, guilt, shame, anger, powerlessness, confusion?

This emotion is the ignition.

Step 2: Trace the Trigger

Now move one layer earlier. What *triggered* the emotion? Was it a word someone said? A facial expression? A tone? A situation that reminded you of something earlier in life?

This is often where the original script lives.

If someone raised their voice and you shut down, the trigger might be the volume, not the content. If you felt dismissed by a coworker and instantly started proving your worth, the trigger might be the perceived rejection — not their actual words.

Write the trigger down. You're reversing the script, frame by frame.

Step 3: Break the Frame

This is the power move.

Every script is based on a belief. Something in you decided, long ago, "When X happens, the only way to be safe/accepted/loved is to do Y."

But most of those beliefs weren't yours to begin with. They were installed through early emotional imprinting, school systems, authority dynamics, or trauma.

Now you test the belief: *Is it true that if I don't respond this way, I'll lose safety or value?*

You'll notice that the belief dissolves under light. You may feel a moment of disorientation — that's the break. The loop has no energy to feed on if you don't respond as expected.

Step 4: Reprogram the Loop

Now you install the new instruction.

Ask yourself: *What would a sovereign version of me choose in this moment, if I didn't feel threatened?*

That's your rewrite.

You're not trying to become robotic or emotionally numb. You're reclaiming authorship. You're choosing the emotion *after* awareness, not being dragged by it without consent.

Use clear phrases like:
- "This emotion is old. I can feel it without obeying it."
- "I recognize the trigger, and I choose differently now."
- "My response is mine. I'm not running their script anymore."

This is not about suppressing emotion. It's about decoding the moment and choosing a new one.

The Hidden Payoff

Most scripts stay alive because they provide a payoff. Even if it's negative, it's predictable. Familiar. Safe.

When you start breaking them, you may feel vulnerable or uncertain. That's growth.

You are not deleting your identity. You are revealing it — beneath the software.

Logic, language, and emotion were never the enemy. They were hijacked. Now you take them back.

Language becomes your tool, not your cage.

Logic becomes your ally, not your jailer.

Emotion becomes your compass, not your leash.

And the game? You stop being the piece on the board.

You become the one who sees it. Moves through it. Rewrites it.

Chapter 2. The Nature of the Script: What Reality Actually Runs On

Scripts as Energy-Sequences: Thought, Emotion, Action, Outcome

Most people believe they make decisions through willpower. They think the life they are living is a result of conscious choices. But what truly drives behavior is not intention alone — it's energy. And that energy follows a precise sequence.

Every script that runs your life is not just mental or emotional. It is energetic. It begins as a subtle shift in frequency and cascades through a predictable chain: thought, emotion, action, outcome. This sequence becomes a loop. That loop becomes identity. And that identity becomes your reality.

Until you decode the energetic architecture of that loop, you stay trapped in outcomes that seem to "just happen," unaware that you are the transmitter. Let's break the chain and rebuild it consciously.

Thought: The Initiation Point

A thought is more than words in your mind. It is an encoded frequency — a pattern that signals what is true, what is possible, and what should be expected. Most thoughts are inherited. They arise from neural grooves carved by repetition, upbringing, trauma, or cultural conditioning.

You don't consciously think them. You *receive* them. And because they've been repeated so many times, they feel like truth.

Examples:
- "It's too late for me."
- "Nothing ever works out."
- "I have to earn everything the hard way."
- "If I rest, I'll fall behind."

These thoughts don't just color your perspective. They generate energy. That energy activates the next layer.

Emotion: The Amplifier

Thoughts are like matches. Emotion is what lights them. When a thought is charged with emotion, it becomes magnetic. It starts to shape your posture, your tone of voice, your expectations, even the way you perceive time.

Emotion is the body's interpretation of energetic truth. If the thought is aligned, the emotion expands you. If the thought is distorted, the emotion contracts you.

Here's the trap: the more times a thought-emotion pairing is repeated, the more familiar it feels. And the more familiar it feels, the more real it seems. If you've experienced rejection and paired it with a thought like "I must not be enough," your system begins to expect and unconsciously recreate rejection just to affirm the script. Emotion then becomes the glue that keeps the thought in place.

Action: The Conduit

Most people believe they act from reason. But by the time you take action, the script has already run through thought and emotion. Action is the surface-level expression of deeper energetic architecture.

If your thought is "I'll be judged," and your emotion is fear, your action will likely be avoidance, silence, or self-sabotage. If your thought is "Success is dangerous," and the emotion is anxiety, your action might be to delay, distract, or overcompensate until you burn out.

This is where people blame their discipline or motivation. But it's not a motivation issue. It's an energetic misalignment. The action isn't weak — it's loyal to the script.

When your actions contradict your desires, it means the sequence is still being driven by an older frequency that hasn't been cleared.

Outcome: The Reinforcement

Every action delivers a result. And every result reinforces the starting point unless interrupted.

This is where the loop tightens. You think a thought, feel an emotion, take action, and then the outcome reflects the exact pattern you were trying to escape. Not because you're cursed — but because energy obeys instruction.

You tell the system, "I always get overlooked," and the system responds, "Understood." So the next opportunity is missed. The loop completes, and the cycle begins again, deeper now because it's "proven."

What you're witnessing is not random life chaos. It is the predictable output of a sequence running below your awareness.

If the outcome reinforces the script, then the only way to break the loop is to consciously disrupt the sequence. That disruption doesn't happen at the surface of action. It happens at the root: the thought and its charge.

Trying to change your behavior without tracing the energetic signal is like repainting a cracked wall without fixing the foundation. It may look different for a moment, but the same fractures will reappear.

How to Reprogram the Sequence

You begin not by resisting the loop, but by mapping it. You observe the chain as it happens without judgment. This is not passive. It is the deepest form of responsibility. You're not trying to be positive. You're becoming precise.

Step 1: Catch the Thought

When something triggers you — a rejection, a delay, a financial setback — pause. Not to suppress the response, but to listen. What is the first sentence your mind fires off? It's usually fast, quiet, and familiar.

You might hear: "See, nothing works." Or, "I'm not ready." Or, "They always do this."

That thought is the script's opening line.

Step 2: Feel the Emotion Without Fusion

Most people collapse into the emotion and let it become identity. But you are training yourself to hold emotion without fusing with it. You feel it, but you do not obey it.

Notice what arises. Fear? Resentment? Shame? Let it surface. Then ask: is this emotion from *now*, or is it echoing something older?

That question alone softens the charge. Emotion starts to unravel when it is met with presence rather than reactivity.

Step 3: Choose a Disruptive Action

The key here is not massive action. It is *incongruent* action. You do something small that breaks the chain. If the old pattern is withdrawal, you speak. If it's aggression, you breathe. If it's people-pleasing, you say no.

You don't need to win. You need to shift.

That one different move sends a new signal. It fractures the energy-sequence and gives you a moment of choice — something the old loop never allowed.

Step 4: Anchor the New Outcome

If you disrupt the sequence, even slightly, a new outcome appears. Maybe the conversation didn't spiral. Maybe the opportunity didn't collapse. Maybe you felt clear instead of drained.

Hold that. It's not luck. It's the reward of energy made conscious.

Now the loop can't close the way it used to. A new groove starts forming. The system registers a different instruction: "I am the initiator. I decide the signal."

Energy as Architecture

The more you run these new sequences, the more your field shifts. Your thoughts don't spiral the same way. Your emotional default state lifts. Your actions start aligning with your actual values. And your outcomes stop feeling like sabotage disguised as fate.

This isn't magic. It's mechanics. Thought, emotion, action, outcome — it's a loop until you rewrite the entry point.

And that rewrite begins in stillness, not force.

There is no need to "try harder." There is a need to see more clearly.

You're not broken. You're encoded. And now, you're the one writing the code.

When you fully grasp that every repeating loop is an energy pattern — not a flaw in your discipline — everything changes. You stop fighting yourself and start observing with precision. And from that clarity, you create with power.

You are not just breaking loops.

You are restoring authorship.

You are returning to the core of how reality responds to you.

And it begins with a thought you actually chose.

Frequency Codes: How Every Choice Emits a Signature

Every decision you make — from what you say in a conversation to what you choose to avoid — carries an energetic signature. It's not the act itself that determines your trajectory, but the *frequency* behind the act. That frequency is what life responds to.

You've likely heard phrases like "alignment" or "vibration," but few understand what they truly mean in practice. These aren't vague spiritual ideas. They are descriptions of how your inner signal codes your external reality.

If you've ever walked into a room and felt tension before anyone spoke, or met someone who radiated peace without saying a word, you've already experienced this. Every human broadcasts frequency. Not metaphorically. Literally. That frequency is the result of your dominant patterns of thought, emotion, and intention. And it is most visible in the way you choose.

The Invisible Signature of Choice

Most people assume their choices are logical. They weigh pros and cons, calculate risks, and move forward. But under the surface, each decision is being shaped by a subtle but powerful field: fear or freedom, scarcity or sufficiency, avoidance or sovereignty.

What you say yes to, what you delay, what you compromise on — all of it encodes a signal.

When you make a choice from anxiety, the frequency that choice carries is not "I want this." It's "I'm afraid of what happens if I don't." That frequency attracts more uncertainty, more pressure, more external control.

When you make a choice from resentment or obligation, it may look generous on the outside. But it's carrying a signature of depletion. Life reflects it by draining your energy or attracting people who expect more than you gave.

On the other hand, when you choose from clarity — even if it's uncomfortable — the frequency emitted is self-trust. That frequency shifts timelines. You may not see results immediately, but you've exited the distortion field that most people live in.

Why Frequency Is Louder Than Words

You can say all the right things. You can visualize, script, and affirm. But if the energy behind your choices is still soaked in doubt, the universe doesn't hear your words. It hears your frequency.

This is why so many people feel like they're doing the work and nothing's changing. They're repeating new affirmations with old patterns. They're setting goals but negotiating with their power in every decision. The frequency hasn't changed — only the language has.

Real transformation begins when you start *feeling* your signal before you act. That's when you stop asking, "Is this the right move?" and start asking, "What's the energy I'm bringing to this move?"

It's not the choice. It's the charge.

And this charge — this signature — is shaping your outcomes, moment by moment.

Detecting Your Current Signature

To begin changing your life, you first need to detect what you're currently broadcasting. This requires honesty without self-judgment. It's not about shame. It's about signal clarity.

Every repeated experience in your life is the echo of a recurring frequency. You don't need to decode the whole pattern all at once. You just need to pause before your next decision and feel: What is the subtle sensation behind this choice?

Tension? Rush? Avoidance? Contraction?

Or: Calm? Strength? Openness?

Even if your mind justifies the decision, your body always knows the signal. You feel it in the stomach, in the breath, in the spine.

The moment you recognize the signal, you reclaim authority. You realize that your reality wasn't happening *to* you — it was answering you.

This awareness is not a mental game. It's a sensory discipline. The more consistently you observe the energetic texture behind your choices, the more accurately you begin to forecast your outcomes. Your life becomes less about control, more about signal alignment.

Frequency isn't just emotional. It is directional. It determines not only how you feel but where you end up. When you shift it, you change the path —

not by force, but by resonance. High-frequency choices resonate with high-frequency outcomes. Not because of magical thinking, but because they create internal coherence. That coherence makes you more decisive, more present, and more willing to act with clarity instead of reacting from confusion.

When you enter a space of congruence — where your thoughts, emotions, and intentions match — the need for external validation diminishes. You stop waiting for proof. You become the proof. And your choices start to leave a different imprint.

The Frequency Recognition Tool

If you want to rewrite the script, you must change the signal. To do that, you first need a way to track it. Below is a simple tool that helps you bring unconscious frequencies into conscious awareness. Use it before a decision, after a conversation, or at the end of your day.

This is not journaling. This is mapping your energetic code.

1. **The Event or Choice**

   Write down what just happened or what you are about to do. Be specific. For example: "Said yes to a client request I didn't really want to do."

2. **Sensory Feedback**

   Immediately scan your body. What are you feeling in your chest, gut, jaw, or spine? Write down the physical sensations without analyzing them. Tension, heaviness, tightness, warmth — any response is data.

3. **Core Frequency Word**

   Choose a word that best captures the energy behind the action. Not the reason, not the story — the *feel*. Examples: pressure, duty, excitement, fear, trust, resentment, confidence.

4. **Expected Outcome Pattern**

   Ask: "What kind of results do I usually get when I operate from this frequency?" Don't guess. Base it on lived patterns. If you often say yes from guilt, what usually follows? If you make bold decisions from certainty, what tends to unfold?

5. **Signal Recalibration**

    If the frequency word doesn't match who you want to be, pause. Imagine acting from the opposite frequency. For example, if the current word is "pressure," what would "power" feel like? You don't need to fake it — just find the smallest action or breath that moves you in that direction.

This tool doesn't require hours. It requires honesty. The more you practice, the more automatic the scan becomes. Soon, you'll start sensing the code before it fully activates. That's when your choices start breaking the loop and forming a new timeline.

Why This Changes Everything

Reality is frequency-responsive. The world reflects your signal more faithfully than your words, hopes, or strategies. When you stop outsourcing your decision-making to logic alone and start tuning into your energetic signal, you're no longer guessing. You're emitting with precision.

Most people unconsciously leak frequency. They give off signals of desperation while trying to appear confident. They broadcast fear while pushing for success. They emit doubt while demanding respect. Then they wonder why the world doesn't respond as they hoped.

When your signal becomes congruent with your intention, things accelerate. Responses become cleaner. Doors open or close with clarity. You attract less chaos, not because the world has changed, but because you're no longer vibrating at the level that invites it.

And when you do encounter friction, you recognize it not as punishment but as signal feedback. Your awareness becomes a tuning fork. Every choice becomes a broadcast. And your life, finally, begins to sound like your own frequency.

You are no longer living by reaction. You're coding the field. Quietly. Powerfully. In real time.

The Script Layers: Outer Reality vs Internal Directive

At the surface, life looks like a series of unrelated events. A job offer. A breakup. An unexpected bill. A casual conversation that changes your trajectory. Most people live reacting to these outer scripts, believing they are navigating an unpredictable world. But when you start looking deeper, patterns begin to appear. Not random. Not chaotic. Scripted.

What feels like "reality" is often a preloaded broadcast. The system feeds you narratives, choices, and consequences based on layers of unexamined programming. These layers don't operate on the same level. They stack — like a hologram, each influencing the next. If you only focus on changing outer conditions, you'll always be one step behind. The real directive is internal. The world follows.

Layer 1: The Surface Script (Outer Reality)

This is what most people mistake for truth. It includes visible events, other people's behavior, social norms, news cycles, and circumstantial triggers. It's the conversation at work, the traffic jam, the rising cost of rent. These elements feel external and fixed, so we chase control. We strategize, overthink, or shrink into compliance trying to "win" a game written by someone else.

But what you experience at this layer is just the echo — not the origin.

Every reaction you have to external circumstances reveals the deeper script that was already playing. The traffic jam didn't create your anger. The breakup didn't create your unworthiness. They activated a script that was already embedded, already rehearsed.

Layer 2: The Emotional Directive (Energetic Imprint)

Below the surface is a dense field of emotional patterning. This is where your nervous system starts calling the shots. These emotional directives are not conscious, but they are loud. You might have learned, very early, that approval equals safety. Or that being unseen protects you. Or that power creates danger. These beliefs aren't always verbal. They live in the body.

So you don't just "choose" your response to the outer world. You broadcast it. Your nervous system becomes a transmitter. And the world responds accordingly.

This is why two people can face the same situation and experience entirely different realities. One interprets a challenge as threat. The other reads it as opportunity. The difference isn't mindset. It's imprint.

Your emotional directive runs the script before your thoughts even arrive. That's why trying to outthink your patterns rarely works. The command was issued before logic had time to speak.

Layer 3: The Internal Directive (Core Script)

At the core of your behavior is something deeper than feeling. It's your internal directive — the silent code you obey without knowing you're obeying it. This layer shapes how much energy you allow yourself to hold, how much risk you tolerate, and how much expansion you can sustain before self-sabotage kicks in.

This is not about belief systems alone. It's about identity-level code.

You may believe you want wealth, but your core script says "money will make you a target." You may say you want love, but your internal directive reads "intimacy equals loss of freedom." Until these deeper codes are updated, no amount of strategy will override the broadcast. You will find yourself stuck in loops that logic cannot explain.

Recognizing these layers is the first step. But to begin working with them directly, you'll need a new kind of attention — one that watches your internal movement without judgment and tracks the signal behind each experience without getting pulled into the drama of the outer script.

To work with these layers, you must start reversing the direction of your attention. Most people react from the outside in. An event triggers an emotion, the emotion justifies an action, and the result becomes the next confirmation of the surface script. This loop reinforces itself endlessly. Your role is to break the loop by tracing the thread in the opposite direction — from outer outcome, back to action, back to emotional directive, and finally to the internal code.

This is not a mental exercise. It's a precision tool for inner pattern recognition. And it begins with conscious reflection.

Trace the Outcome Backward

Start with something recent that didn't go the way you wanted. Maybe a job offer fell through, a conversation turned tense, or you missed a major opportunity. Don't focus on what happened — focus on what you felt. Track your emotional response without judging it. Was there frustration? Fear? Shame? Resistance?

From that emotion, ask: what action did I take because I felt this? Did I pull back? Overcompensate? Avoid? Fight?

Now go one level deeper: what belief or internal truth was silently running in the background? The one you didn't say out loud, but followed anyway. Maybe it sounded like: *"If I speak up, I'll lose the chance."* Or *"I'm not the kind of person who gets picked."* Or *"Too much success is dangerous."*

This is where you find the script. Not in the story — in the directive.

Decoding the Directive with Precision

The internal directive often reveals itself through patterns of self-protection. Wherever you habitually avoid discomfort, risk, or visibility, there is a script trying to keep you safe — even if it limits you.

The key isn't to fight it. The key is to recognize the outdated logic behind it.

A script formed when you were 8 years old might have made sense in a household where love was conditional. But now that same directive sabotages relationships by shutting down vulnerability. You didn't consciously choose this. But until it's brought into awareness, it continues to run silently.

Your job is not to eliminate the emotion. Your job is to question the directive beneath it.

Ask:
- *What would have to be true for this pattern to make sense?*
- *What threat is this script trying to neutralize?*
- *Where else in my life does this logic appear, uninvited?*

You'll start seeing the layers stacked: outer reality reflecting your action, which came from emotion, which came from an old code trying to protect something that no longer needs protection.

From Recognition to Rewrite

Once identified, the directive can be rewritten. But not with wishful thinking. You must offer your system a *safer* alternative — not just a more positive one. If the old code was about avoiding pain, the new directive must include a path to safety that allows expansion, not threat.

This often begins by creating small experiences that contradict the old pattern. If your script says, *"Being seen is dangerous,"* then the rewrite begins with low-risk moments of visibility that your nervous system can tolerate. Not force. Not performance. Just calibrated challenge.

With time, these small proofs accumulate. The directive loosens. The emotion no longer spikes. The action shifts. And the outer script begins to change, because it's no longer being fed the same signal.

Living from the Deepest Layer

The power of this model is not just in analysis. It's in sovereignty. When you live from the deepest layer, you no longer wait for life to grant you permission. You no longer try to manipulate the outer layer with effort or performance. You broadcast a different signal — and the script must follow. Because what you emit shapes what you experience. And once you become the one who writes from within, no outer script has the power to dictate your path.

Chapter 3. The Hijacking: Who Wrote the Script You're Living Now

Cultural Imprinting and Subconscious Inheritance

You were not born a blank slate. Long before you formed your first conscious thought, your mind was absorbing patterns. These were not just behaviors you mimicked from your parents or phrases you heard on TV. They were codes — invisible templates etched into your subconscious by culture, lineage, language, and history. And most of them were never yours to begin with.

What you call "you" is, in part, a layered collection of inherited responses. Some were passed down biologically, encoded in the nervous system through generations of adaptation and survival. Others were transferred energetically or emotionally — the aftermath of wars, famines, migrations, religious trauma, or ancestral silence. And many more were absorbed simply by growing up within the constructs of your society: school systems, media, laws, expectations, myths, taboos.

The reason your life often feels strangely shaped — like you're living someone else's blueprint — is because, in many ways, you are.

What Culture Imprints Before You Choose

By the time you were seven, your subconscious mind had already formed its primary operating system. In that short window, you absorbed unspoken rules about gender roles, success, love, worth, punishment, and possibility. You saw how people like you were treated, what was rewarded, what was dismissed, and what was considered dangerous to express.

If you were raised in a high-pressure environment, achievement might have become your core strategy for safety. If you were taught to be polite above all else, you may still silence your voice even when something matters. If your culture equated sacrifice with virtue, you may feel guilt for choosing ease or pleasure.

These aren't rational choices. They are subconscious inheritances. They form the *scripts* that feel so familiar you mistake them for truth.

Even rebellion often follows the same pattern — reacting to the same core rules, just in reverse. You're still trapped inside the same imprint.

The Hidden Layer of Collective Narratives

Beyond family and upbringing, there are collective cultural scripts that influence how you see the world and yourself. These are often harder to detect because they seem "normal." But normal is often a collective agreement to stay unconscious.

For example, Western culture subtly glorifies burnout as proof of value. Productivity is often equated with morality. You may feel ashamed for resting, even when exhausted. That's not your individual flaw — it's cultural conditioning.

Or take the narrative around money: if your society frames wealth as inherently corrupt, you may find yourself repelling abundance while claiming to want it. If love is framed as something you must "earn," your relationships may become stages where you perform instead of connect.

These narratives are powerful because they operate below the surface. You don't argue with them — you live inside them.

The same is true of inherited shame. In some lineages or regions, certain topics are culturally suppressed: sexuality, emotional expression, spiritual intuition. Children raised in those environments often internalize a deep-seated fear of being "too much" or "not enough." They adapt by muting their true selves.

Over time, this creates a split between the authentic self and the adapted identity. And that split becomes the breeding ground for internal conflict, confusion, or the sense that no matter what you do, it never feels fully *you*.

Inheritance Is Not Destiny

What you've inherited may explain your patterns, but it doesn't justify your stagnation. Awareness begins the process of reclaiming authorship. But to truly free yourself, you must do more than understand the scripts — you must question who wrote them, who benefits from them staying hidden, and what your life would become without them.

The moment you ask, "Whose voice is this in my head?" you are no longer trapped in it. That moment of interruption, even if brief, breaks the trance of inheritance. And it reveals the truth: these scripts do not belong to you.

They were placed there, layer by layer, like graffiti on clean glass. The clarity is still underneath, waiting to be uncovered.

Some of the scripts were designed to protect. Others were designed to suppress. Not all inheritance is malicious, but most of it is unconscious. And the unconscious repeats itself by default. Unless interrupted, you will live out the same emotional responses, thought patterns, and relational dynamics that were modeled for you, even if you swore you never would.

This is why awareness alone is not enough. You can know that your father's silence shaped your fear of rejection. You can understand that your culture's avoidance of grief created your numbness. But unless you feel those buried experiences and confront the emotions underneath them, the imprint remains active. It lives not just in your thoughts, but in your body, your nervous system, and your reactions.

The inheritance becomes invisible precisely because it feels internal. But what feels internal is often just deeply conditioned. This is the illusion of identity. You assume that if it's inside you, it must be you. That's the trap.

Liberation starts with remembering that the subconscious is not your enemy. It's a survival mechanism. It took on these patterns because it thought they would help you belong, stay safe, be loved, or avoid punishment. The subconscious doesn't care if the pattern is true. It only cares if the pattern once worked.

The problem is, your context has changed — but the pattern hasn't. You are no longer a child. You are no longer helpless. But the imprint doesn't update itself automatically. It must be reprogrammed.

This is not about therapy, though therapy may help. This is about reclaiming sovereignty over the internal architecture that governs your perception. It means rewriting emotional responses at the root, not managing them at the surface. It means identifying whose shame you're carrying, whose fear you mistake for your own, and what beliefs no longer serve the person you are becoming.

It also requires a different kind of courage: the willingness to disappoint the expectations you inherited. You may find that your expansion threatens the identity your family clung to for safety. You may feel like a traitor to your culture when you stop playing the role it assigned you. But that discomfort is not a sign you're doing something wrong. It's a sign that you're leaving the trance.

Every lineage contains unfinished business. What is not resolved is repeated. You are either the continuation of the old script, or the interruption that rewrites it.

When you choose to become that interruption — not just intellectually, but emotionally, energetically, behaviorally — you collapse the loop. You stop being the echo and become the author. And that is what breaks generational hypnosis.

You do not need to know every detail of your ancestry or cultural history to begin this process. What matters is that you recognize when you're reenacting a pattern that does not align with your current truth. Every time you pause and feel the deeper choice beneath the reflex, you rewrite the code. Every time you refuse to obey an unspoken rule that keeps you small, you upgrade the frequency. And every time you live in a way that honors your actual essence, you heal what those before you could not.

This is how you become the end of one story and the beginning of another — not by effort or rebellion alone, but by conscious inheritance. You choose what stays. You release what doesn't. You reclaim what was buried. And for the first time, the script becomes yours.

The Silent Coders: Media, Schooling, and Mass Reality Loops

Most people don't realize they're being programmed because the programmers don't wear uniforms or hold weapons. They hold microphones, chalkboards, and screens. They appear in classrooms, news studios, and movie sets. The silent coders of reality aren't the ones who shout orders. They are the ones who define normal. And when something is normalized, it becomes invisible.

This invisibility is the most dangerous form of control. It doesn't need to convince you with force. It only needs to shape your perception of what's real, acceptable, or desirable. And once it does that, you'll script your own behavior to match the illusion.

It starts early. School doesn't just teach you math and grammar. It teaches you obedience to bells, rules, and authority. You learn that asking too many questions makes you "difficult." That failure is shameful. That memorization is more important than understanding. The point isn't education. It's domestication.

You are trained to perform, to please, to meet expectations. And once that framework is in place, media steps in to keep it active. It shows you what a good life looks like, who is desirable, what success means, and how happiness should feel. None of these definitions are neutral. They are engineered to keep you buying, watching, fearing, striving, and comparing.

This is the mass loop: a cycle of constant dissatisfaction fueled by external standards. It's not just the ads. It's the framing of stories, the repetition of slogans, the emotional tone of headlines. You are not just absorbing content. You are absorbing frequency. The emotional signature of the content becomes part of your own baseline energy.

Most people don't question it because it all seems so "normal." But this normalcy is synthetic. It is a curated version of life that keeps the population predictable and reactive. When people believe the same fears, chase the same dreams, and follow the same rules, they become easier to manage — and easier to sell to.

The coding is subtle. A sitcom laugh track tells you when something is funny, even if you didn't laugh. A news anchor's tone tells you what to be afraid of, even if you didn't notice. A film score tells you what to feel before the scene begins. This emotional scaffolding is everywhere, shaping your responses before you even think.

And this is not just a passive influence. It rewires the brain. Neuroscience confirms that repetition builds neural pathways. What you see often becomes what you believe. What you believe becomes how you perceive. And how you perceive becomes how you live.

By adulthood, most people have internalized thousands of hours of scripted narratives that were not designed for their sovereignty, but for their compliance. The saddest part is that they don't know where their own thoughts end and the programming begins. They think they are making choices, but the choices are pre-filtered through invisible constraints.

It's not just the message. It's the absence of other messages. What is never said, never shown, never named — that's part of the control too. Certain worldviews are excluded altogether, not by censorship, but by design. If a possibility is never presented, you don't consider it. If a model of reality is never shown, you assume it doesn't exist.

And so you live in a mental sandbox, thinking it's the entire world.

The only way out is awareness. You must start seeing the structure behind the content. You must begin to notice not just what is being said, but how it's being said — and what it's training you to feel or believe.

Once you begin to see that most of what you believe was implanted through repetition, authority, and emotional cues, the next step is not panic. It's precision. Awareness must become a tool, not a vague idea. You need to map where the loops begin, how they enter your system, and how they shape your decisions, your energy, and your identity.

Let's begin with a practical awareness checklist. You can use this tool to catch the coders in action — and more importantly, to prevent unconscious absorption. Each question is a trigger for clarity.

1. What emotional state is being induced?

Every piece of media carries a frequency. Does it create urgency? Fear? Guilt? Envy? If the emotional tone is strong, ask yourself who benefits from you feeling that. Emotional manipulation is the quickest way to bypass your logic.

2. What is being framed as normal?

When a character in a series drinks heavily after a breakup, or spends recklessly to feel better, it's often shown as relatable. But repetition of dysfunctional behavior dressed up as entertainment is a subtle form of normalization. Ask: is this a pattern I want in my field?

3. What is being left out?

Often, the most powerful form of control is omission. Whose voices are not included? What perspectives are never presented? What solutions are never mentioned? Absence creates blind spots, and blind spots maintain loops.

4. Is the message appealing to your fear or desire?

When you're being shown images of scarcity, doom, urgency, or ideal lifestyles, check what part of your nervous system is being activated. Are you being drawn into fight, flight, or freeze? Or into craving, grasping, and unworthiness?

5. Does this encourage thinking — or obedience?

A true message expands your ability to reflect and question. A loop message pressures you to act quickly, conform, or pick from a pre-selected set of reactions. The moment you feel your autonomy shrinking, pause.

6. Who profits if you believe this?

This question can cut through almost anything. Follow the incentives. If a belief leads you to buy, vote, submit, or chase a certain outcome — and someone benefits from that — your perception has likely been shaped.

Once you begin using this checklist consistently, the entire field of input starts to shift. You no longer watch or scroll passively. You start to notice that entertainment is often a delivery system for values. That algorithms don't just suggest content. They curate identity.

Your nervous system, over time, stops reacting on command. You reclaim the capacity to hold a thought without becoming it. You become less programmable. This is the first real exit from the mass loop: not isolation, not rejection, but sovereign filtration.

Rewriting the internal code starts by withdrawing consent from the external ones. That doesn't mean you never engage with media or information. It means you stop surrendering your baseline energy to it. You become the one who decides what enters your field — and what doesn't.

This is not just mental hygiene. It's energetic sovereignty. The loops you absorb become the frequencies you emit. And the frequencies you emit attract more of the same. This is how unconscious programming compounds over time — but also how conscious filtration breaks the cycle. The silent coders win when you forget you're being coded. But once you begin to see the fingerprints behind the frame, the spell loses power. You don't need to destroy the system. You only need to stop running on it.

In the chapters ahead, we'll go deeper into how to actively rewrite the scripts inside you — but this awareness checklist is the gate. It trains your perception to move from passive to precise. And once your perception sharpens, your power returns.

Not gradually. Instantly.

The Energetic Parasites that Feed on Your Compliance

There's a reason you feel exhausted after certain interactions, drained by seemingly harmless habits, or strangely low after consuming what others call "normal." Most people chalk it up to stress, poor sleep, or a bad mood. But beneath those surface explanations lies something more precise — a network of subtle, energetic parasites that feed not on your body, but on your compliance.

These parasites don't look like what you might expect. They are not physical organisms. They don't announce their presence. They operate silently, through patterns of attention, thought, emotion, and obedience. And the fuel they depend on is your unconscious participation.

They thrive in environments where people obey without question. Where social expectations override personal truth. Where guilt, shame, and fear are mistaken for responsibility. Where saying no feels unsafe. Where survival depends on staying small, agreeable, or invisible.

Energetic parasites are real. Not in the sense of science fiction, but in the sense of frequency dynamics. Every time you betray your own knowing to avoid discomfort, a small leak opens. That leak becomes a channel. That channel becomes a loop. And over time, that loop becomes a feeding ground.

If you've ever walked away from a conversation feeling like you lost something — not just time, but clarity, confidence, or vitality — you've felt it. If you've agreed to something you didn't believe in just to avoid conflict, and then couldn't sleep that night, you've felt it. If you've numbed yourself with distractions, and then found yourself more tired than before, you've felt it.

These drains are not accidental. They are patterned. And once you begin to map them, you'll see that they form part of a much larger structure.

Let's begin to bring this out of the abstract. You don't need to believe in metaphysics to notice that energy can be taken, redirected, and depleted. You only need to notice how you feel before and after specific interactions, behaviors, and internal compromises. That's your map.

To begin identifying where energy is leaking and where parasites may be feeding, you'll use the Energy Leak Identification Tool. This is not about fear. It's about precision. You're not a victim of these leaks — you're the architect of your consent. And that means you can withdraw it.

This tool involves three phases of observation:

1. Scan Your Energy Landscape

Choose three recent situations where you left feeling drained, foggy, irritated, or strangely tired. Write them down in detail. What happened? Who was involved? What did you agree to? What did you suppress?

Now go deeper. In each of those situations, ask yourself:
- Did I override a boundary?
- Did I avoid expressing something I knew to be true?
- Did I absorb someone else's emotion, expectation, or chaos?
- Did I try to manage the other person's perception of me instead of being honest?

Most people find patterns immediately. Certain environments, people, or roles consistently lead to depletion. These are your energetic red flags. They're not always obvious. Sometimes it's not the loud conflict that drains you, but the quiet agreement you didn't even notice making.

2. Track the Internal Compliance Mechanism

What allowed the drain to happen? Was it a fear of rejection? A need to be liked? A belief that saying no would make you unsafe, unloved, or alone?

These are the internal contracts you've signed — often long ago, without realizing it. They are the root systems of energetic parasites. The parasites don't create the fear. They feed on the energy it releases when you obey it.

This is where most people stop looking. They notice the fatigue, maybe even the guilt or resentment, but they never trace it back to the moment they gave their power away. That moment always has a signature. It's not always loud. It's often quiet, automatic, habitual. And that's why it's profitable — for them.

The world you live in runs on the energy of those who comply. Systems don't sustain themselves. They require participants who follow instructions without conscious evaluation. This is the soil in which energetic parasites thrive. They don't need to convince you they exist. They only need you to keep betraying yourself in small, regular doses.

Now you begin to take your energy back.

3. Reverse the Leak

For each of the three situations you wrote down earlier, ask yourself one more question: what would withdrawal of consent have looked like?

Not the dramatic version — not shouting, not burning bridges. Just the quiet, firm refusal to abandon yourself. The truth spoken plainly. The silence honored instead of filled. The pause allowed instead of overridden. This is where the parasite can no longer feed.

When you start honoring the signal of depletion as a sign of misalignment, you stop treating fatigue as a flaw and start using it as feedback. Every energy leak is a clue. Every moment of internal dissonance points to a place where you've been programmed to prioritize compliance over clarity.

The shift doesn't require you to fight anything. In fact, most of these systems expect your resistance. They are designed to absorb it, to let you scream and vent and protest as long as you return to the role when you're done. What they can't absorb is your stillness. Your awareness. Your refusal to play the script at all.

Energetic sovereignty begins the moment you stop reacting and start observing.

You might think this is small. That choosing not to answer a message, or pausing before saying yes, or declining to explain yourself, is insignificant. But that's the recalibration. You are removing permission in micro-moments. And each one rewrites the energetic contract.

When you do this consistently, the parasites lose access.

You'll notice people start reacting differently to you. Some might get angry. Some might distance themselves. Some might try harder to pull you back into old roles. That's not because you've done anything wrong. It's because they can no longer plug into your frequency without consent. You've closed the leak.

If you want to track this over time, create a personal Energy Leak Log. Each week, document the moments where you either gave your energy away or chose to keep it. Don't judge yourself. Just notice. You'll begin to see how certain patterns dissolve the moment they're seen clearly.

This work doesn't just give you back energy. It gives you back agency. Because what you once thought was personality — the tendency to people-please, over-explain, say yes when you meant no — was often just an adaptation. A script written by the fear of being too much, too honest, too sovereign.

You're not too much. You're simply untethering from what was feeding off your compliance.

As you begin to see how energy moves, you'll recognize that true power doesn't come from dominating others or shielding yourself constantly. It comes from discernment. From knowing what's yours, and what was never meant to enter. From choosing where your energy flows, rather than having it siphoned silently.

You can't always control the environments you walk into. But you can control whether you remain open or closed. Whether you align or submit. Whether you feed the loop or withdraw from it.

This is how you exit the parasitic ecosystem. Not with noise, but with precision. Not with rebellion for rebellion's sake, but with a grounded refusal to abandon yourself again.

You begin by noticing. Then by naming. And finally, by reclaiming what was always yours: your own frequency, undistorted, uncolonized, and fully yours to direct.

Part II. Disrupting the Code of the Game

There comes a moment when seeing is no longer enough. Awareness, by itself, becomes a trap — a hall of mirrors where you recognize the patterns, the loops, the silent directives, but feel powerless to stop them. You understand the programming, yet still feel it moving through your actions, decisions, and emotions. This is the limbo where many get stuck: fully awake, yet still entranced.

That's not your path.

This part of the journey is not about observation. It's about interruption. Precision. Interference. You're no longer just the witness of the script. You're becoming the disruptor of it.

Disrupting the code of the game is not an act of destruction. It's not about fighting systems or resisting every structure. That's still reaction. That's still the game. Disruption, in this context, means severing the automatic loop between stimulus and response. It means cutting the cord between inherited thought and repeated behavior. It means shifting your energetic and cognitive posture so deeply that the old scripts no longer find a place to land.

In Part I, you were decoding. Now you are recoding.

You'll begin to notice how reality changes not by force, but by the subtle recalibration of what you allow. You'll see how language, perception, and memory all operate as access points — and how slight edits in awareness can completely reroute an outcome. You'll start intervening not just after the fact, but before the pattern even begins. This is where timing becomes power.

But don't expect comfort here. Disrupting the code means stepping out of roles that once felt safe. It means holding silence when your old self would have filled the space. It means making choices that don't offer instant validation. You're not just learning how to act differently — you're becoming someone the script can no longer predict.

This section gives you tools, but not in the way you've been trained to expect. These are not formulas or surface-level techniques. They are weapons of perception. Lenses that expose the false logic running in the background. Shifts that make manipulation collapse before it takes form. And above all, practices that reroute your nervous system, your language, and your attention so that you stop being a match for control-based frequencies.

The code you're disrupting isn't just outside of you. It's been internalized. Worn like a second skin. That's what makes this part difficult. You'll confront the voices that feel like yours but were planted years ago. You'll hear the phrases in your head that were never truly your own. You'll feel the pull to revert — and this time, you'll pause instead.

That pause is the crack. The fracture in the script. The entry point to something unscripted, alive, and sovereign.

You don't need to dismantle your entire identity overnight. You only need to keep interrupting the loop long enough for something else to emerge. That's the frequency of this part: interruption with intelligence. Disruption with direction. Precision over performance.

And you'll begin to feel it — not as theory, but as frequency. The feeling of walking differently. Thinking with more space. Acting with less compulsion. Speaking from center, not from defense.

Disruption isn't rage. It's clarity.

And clarity is what the system fears most.

Now you move. Not on autopilot, not as a reaction, but as the one who sees the code, breaks the sequence, and rewrites the entire field from within.

Chapter 4. Access Points: Where to Intercept and Rewire the Script

The Three Moments Where Script Can Be Cut or Edited

If life unfolds like a script, then your greatest power is knowing exactly where the script can be interrupted. Most people assume change requires a grand decision or total life upheaval. In reality, the shift begins at micro-moments. Tiny forks in the road where awareness can be inserted like a blade, severing the automatic loop between perception and reaction.

There are only three true points where a script can be cut, redirected, or rewritten. Every transformation, no matter how complex, begins at one of these junctures. Once you can identify these entry points in real time, you stop feeling like a passive actor. You begin shaping the sequence from within.

These three moments don't require perfection. They require precision. The ability to recognize the space before movement, the silence before speech, the feeling before action. Once you know how to notice them, they become access keys to a deeper version of you — the one who chooses, not just performs.

Let's map the first.

1. The Pre-Thought Sensation: Cutting the Script Before It Speaks

The earliest moment a script can be edited doesn't begin with a thought. It begins with a sensation. A tightening in the chest, a flutter in the gut, a slight clench in the jaw. These are not symptoms. They're signals. Most people override them automatically, thinking these sensations are too subtle to matter. But this is where the original code embeds.

Long before you reach for a behavior, your nervous system already decided what feels safe, familiar, or possible. That decision doesn't arise in words. It begins with energy. If you only intervene at the level of thought, you're already late. You're intercepting the symptom, not the source.

This first moment — the somatic flicker — is where loops are born. If left unobserved, it triggers the usual chain: thought, emotion, behavior, consequence. But when met with stillness, this same sensation becomes a pivot point. You don't need to decode it intellectually. You simply need to pause. Breathe. Observe the signal without obeying it. In that pause, the old command loses force.

The most powerful disruptions happen before language gets involved. When you can notice the script trying to take hold before it finds words, you've already begun rewriting your internal architecture.

2. The Inner Commentary: Cutting the Script During Narration

Once the sensation has been ignored, the second moment arrives: the internal monologue. This is the story that wraps itself around the feeling. It sounds like logic, but it's usually camouflage. A script needs justification to survive. So it generates a narrative that feels true, but is often recycled from past identity patterns.

This commentary isn't neutral. It's directional. It moves you toward a specific response, shaped by memory, culture, trauma, and prior reinforcement. It tells you why you're right to be afraid. Why you should withdraw. Why you need to act fast. Or why you always mess it up.

Most people live from this narrative space. They don't question it, because it sounds like their own voice. But the voice is rarely original. It's stitched together from years of silent conditioning and emotional repetition.

To edit the script here, you don't need to fight the voice. You need to expose it. Hear it without identifying with it. Track it without feeding it. Ask, "Whose words are these, really?" The script cannot run without your agreement. Withdraw that agreement, and its power crumbles.

This is the space where you install a different frequency — not by force, but by choice. You don't need to argue with the thought. You only need to refuse its authority.

The third moment emerges not before or during thought, but after the action has already begun. This is the behavioral pivot point. It's the space within the act, where momentum is strong, but awareness can still be inserted. Most people believe once a behavior is triggered, it must play out entirely. That belief alone keeps the script intact.

But there is always a window mid-action, even if it's small. A moment inside the habit loop where you can interrupt the cascade. It might be a breath in the middle of an argument, a pause just before sending the message, a sudden awareness of posture or tone. These moments are not dramatic. They are quiet, but decisive. When you catch the pattern mid-flight, you begin to retrieve authority from the very system that trained you to obey.

This third moment is particularly powerful because it proves something radical: change does not require anticipation. You don't need to be perfectly prepared. You only need to wake up for a split second while inside the pattern. That flash of presence rewrites more than all the resolutions made from the outside.

Each of these three entry points reveals a different relationship with your own awareness. The first is before the script forms. The second is while it narrates. The third is as it unfolds. Together, they form a kind of map — a temporal territory where sovereignty can be reclaimed in real time. And because these moments exist on a loop, you will encounter them again and again. Mastery comes not from catching them all at once, but from building sensitivity to each phase and training your system to respond with precision.

These are not just abstract ideas. They are doors. Every door you notice grants you a choice. And every choice you make that breaks the automatic sequence strengthens a new timeline — one no longer built from repetition, but from authorship.

There is a hidden gift in these moments. Not just the ability to shift action, but the ability to see yourself from a different altitude. To move from being inside the code to becoming the one who sees the code. This is the real beginning of freedom. Not freedom from discomfort or effort, but freedom from unconscious obedience.

You don't need to fix everything at once. You only need to see where the edits are possible. Choose one point. Train your attention there. Instead of reacting to the full drama of the script, begin watching for the exact second the light flickers. That flicker is your opening. It is not theoretical. It is real, and it repeats.

To live differently, you don't need more information. You need to meet the moment where the sequence bends. And once you do, even once, the script loses its monopoly. You begin to remember what it feels like to move from clarity, not compulsion. From presence, not programming.

You are not just an actor within the story. You are the one who notices the breath before the line is delivered. That breath is where reality is rewritten. The three moments are not rare. They are everywhere. But only those who train their perception will ever see them. And only those who see them can decide what comes next.

Interrupting the Thought Loop Before It Manifests

Most people live in reaction to thoughts they never consciously chose. These thoughts feel like their own because they happen inside their mind, in their voice, with their vocabulary. But in truth, the majority of these mental loops are old downloads — inherited, repeated, conditioned, and unquestioned. They arise with familiar emotional undertones, reactivating stories that have been recycled for years. And because thought precedes perception, and perception shapes experience, these loops are not innocent. They sculpt reality.

The most dangerous thoughts are not the loudest ones. They are the subtle, habitual, familiar scripts that reinforce limitation. "That won't work," "I'm not ready," "They'll reject me," "I always mess this up." These phrases don't need to shout. They whisper just enough to adjust your decisions, lower your frequency, and keep you playing a smaller game. And when repeated often enough, they embed into your sense of identity, blending seamlessly with who you think you are.

To disrupt this, you cannot wait for the thought to finish. You must become faster than your own internal narrator. That means building the ability to recognize the *feeling* of a looping thought before it has finished forming into words. All thought, especially habitual thought, carries a signature. A texture. A rhythm. Learn to detect that energetic fingerprint. It is always slightly tight, slightly anxious, slightly fast. It constricts the body even before it completes the sentence.

Once you can recognize that signal, you are no longer trapped inside the thought. You are standing next to it, observing it. That shift is everything. From inside the loop, you are the script. From outside the loop, you are the coder.

The goal is not to stop all thinking. Thought itself is not the enemy. What we interrupt is *mechanical thought* — the kind that runs on auto-play, dictated by unresolved emotion and unverified belief. The kind that loops without innovation. That is the pattern to intercept. And to do so, we need a precise point of intervention.

That point is the microsecond of *pre-thought*. Not quite silence, not quite language. A subtle tension that announces the approach of a familiar pattern. Most people miss it, because they are too fused with the thought to notice. But if you slow down your awareness and place it just before the mind starts narrating, you can sense the activation.

This is where the Thought Disruption Protocol begins.

First, stillness. Not dramatic meditation. Just a pause — even one breath. The nervous system needs a crack in the rhythm. That space gives your perception a moment to return to the present. Once you detect the signal of an old loop rising — even if you don't yet know what the content is — pause. You've already started the reprogramming.

Next, name it. Not as a judgment, but as a label. "Loop detected." "Old script." "Not mine." By naming the loop, you separate identity from pattern. This is critical. The thought wants to convince you that it *is* you. Naming it shows it is *not*.

Finally, engage the alternative. Not a forced affirmation. Not a fake mantra. A *real choice*. One thought that feels like it comes from *now*, not from the archive. One thought that feels slightly clearer, slightly more open, slightly more true. It does not have to be perfect. It only needs to be disruptive.

Let that replacement thought generate a new feeling, even briefly. That is what cuts the loop. Not the content, but the shift in energetic pattern. When a new feeling emerges, the neural pathway begins to reroute. Repetition of this process is what rewires the script completely.

The nervous system needs new data to operate differently. It doesn't believe words alone. It believes pattern. And the only way to change the pattern is through experience. So every time you catch the loop before it completes, and you insert a real-time shift — even a small one — you're training the system to respond from presence, not programming.

Some loops will dissolve quickly. Others will cling harder. The more a thought is tied to emotional residue, the more persistent it may be. This is not a sign of failure. It is a sign that there is still energy invested in the story. Sometimes it will surface as discomfort, irritation, or boredom when you try to shift it. That is the parasite protecting its feed. Recognize the resistance as evidence that the process is working.

You are not only breaking a thought. You are breaking a frequency. And frequency has memory. Which is why loops feel like "you" — because they have played long enough to shape your emotional and behavioral identity. Interrupting the loop interrupts the emotional payoff. And every payoff removed is energy reclaimed.

Reclamation is not loud. It is subtle, almost imperceptible at first. But over time, your internal space becomes less crowded. You begin to feel when a thought is about to arise — not by its content, but by its signature. And you meet it not with obedience, but with discernment.

A moment of breath. A name. A new choice.

That is the pulse of freedom. Not dramatic. Not theatrical. Quiet. Consistent. Alive.

There will be days when the loop wins. Let it. Watch it. Let it play through like a song you're tired of hearing. But don't dance to it. Don't obey it. Just note it. The act of conscious witnessing is enough to weaken its grip. Each time you watch without feeding it emotion, you starve the mechanism. And the pattern loses its charge.

Then, redirect. Not to something idealistic. Not to fantasy. Redirect to what is *now*. What is *real*. What is *yours*. Even a small question like "What else is possible right now?" can fracture the rigidity of the loop. It returns you to authorship. And authorship is what reprograms reality.

When your thoughts no longer spiral automatically, your choices become sovereign. Your perception expands. Your energy is no longer burned maintaining false narratives. Instead, it becomes available to create new ones.

This is how you become the coder of the script, not just the character inside it. You no longer react from a story you inherited. You create from a signal you tuned yourself to. The mind is no longer the loudest voice in the room. It becomes one of many tools. You decide when it speaks. And you choose what it serves.

The loop, once disrupted consistently, loses its claim over your identity. The neural grooves fade. The energetic patterns soften. The emotional charge dissolves. You start thinking from clarity, not from conditioning. That is the power of intercepting thought before it manifests. It's not just a technique. It's a form of self-liberation.

You've interrupted thought. You've interrupted frequency. And now, you're free to transmit something new.

How to Identify Real vs Programmed Desires

Not every desire you feel is yours.

Some were whispered into you by parents who couldn't meet their own. Others were coded into you by a system that needed your compliance to function. A few came from comparison, wrapped in the image of someone who seemed to be winning. Many were shaped in your early moments of needing approval, safety, or love. They were survival choices, not sovereign ones.

The problem is, most people live their entire lives chasing those echoes, believing them to be their true calling.

Real desire feels alive in the body. It has a pulse, a gravity. It moves you before it makes sense. It does not always feel safe or familiar. Sometimes it makes no logical sense at all, which is why many discard it early. But real desire does not require explanation. It only requires presence. It doesn't feed off validation. It's not loud. It's consistent.

Programmed desire, on the other hand, is performative. It knows exactly what to say. It fits the model. It sounds just like the voice in your head that wants to be seen, applauded, or safe. It often arrives with justification already built in: "I want this because it's what success looks like." Or "If I get this, then I'll finally feel secure." It's deeply conditional. It leans heavily on future payoff and tends to disappear once it's achieved.

The easiest way to spot programmed desire is to look at its fuel source. If the engine is guilt, fear, or comparison, it's not yours. If you feel more addicted to the image of having it than to the actual experience of living it, it's not yours. If you feel you must *prove* something by getting it, it's not yours.

But to go deeper, you need to do more than evaluate what you want. You need to dissect it.

Desire Dissection Exercise

Take a single desire you've been chasing — one that has followed you for years or one that surfaced more recently but with intensity. Don't filter. Just name it. Maybe it's to build a business, to be wealthy, to be famous, to heal, to be in a perfect relationship, to move away, to live freely.

Now break it open.

Start with this question: *Where did I first get the idea that this was important?*
Let yourself trace it. Was it in childhood? Was it modeled by someone you admired? Was it the opposite of what you had? Go slow. Let the memory surface without editing it.

Then ask: *What emotion do I associate with having it?*
Is it relief? Is it power? Is it love? Is it escape?

Now go even deeper: *What part of me believes that I am not already allowed to feel that emotion now?*

This is where the real programming lives — in the assumption that some part of you must achieve, perform, or become something in order to be whole. If the desire is rooted in that assumption, it may not be coming from your truth. It may be a script.

Real desire survives scrutiny. It may evolve as you evolve, but it never evaporates under truth. It has its own rhythm. You don't need to chase it to keep it alive. You meet it by becoming the version of yourself who can hold it without distortion.

One of the biggest shifts happens when you stop asking, *What do I want?* and start asking, *What wants to move through me?* This shift removes the egoic filter. It removes the need to perform or justify. Instead, it invites the body, the intuition, and the deeper mind into the conversation.

You start noticing that real desires often come quietly, like soft signals. You feel drawn to something without fanfare. There's no performance attached. No race to arrive. Just a feeling that something is *yours to walk into*.

These are the desires that restructure reality. They create a gravitational field that organizes your life differently. You don't have to convince yourself to keep going. You become willing to lose who you thought you were in order to follow where it leads.

This is why programmed desires often fail to satisfy even when achieved. You got the result, but you didn't get the *feeling* you thought would come with it. Because it was never about the goal. It was about compensating for something unresolved inside you.

That's how the loop works. You chase something that isn't yours. You don't feel the completion you expected. So you raise the stakes or shift the target, thinking *this time* it will feel different. But if the source of the desire was false, no destination will ever feel true.

To escape this cycle, you must train yourself to tune into the resonance of a desire before acting on it. This means sensing the *texture* of the desire in your body, in your nervous system, in your breath. Real desire expands you. Even when it terrifies you, it still feels like it opens a door. Programmed desire contracts you. It feels tight, demanding, pressured. It carries the energy of "not enough yet."

You begin rewriting the code not by force, but by precision. You become a tracker of signals. A detector of distortion. You move slower, but every move is real. You don't override doubt with hustle. You pause and investigate. You don't leap into action just because the world applauds the dream. You ask yourself if it's yours. If it's not, you release it. Not with shame, but with clarity.

This is one of the most radical moves in a system built on obedience. To want what you actually want. To move from the place inside you that has never been domesticated by fear, expectation, or conditioning. That place is not flashy. It does not make promises. But it is where your life becomes yours again.

What emerges from that space is rare. It doesn't mimic anyone else. It doesn't seek applause. It simply *fits*. Not in the eyes of others, but in the quiet knowing inside you. And when you act from that place, your choices carry a different frequency. One that can't be manipulated. One that can't be sold back to you. One that leads you out of the loop and into a life that actually reflects your signal.

That's the moment you stop chasing desire and start transmitting it.

Chapter 5. Timeline Drift: Why You're Always in the Wrong Layer of Reality

Parallel Scripts and the Myth of "One Life"

Most people walk through life with the quiet assumption that there's only one version of their story. One path, one timeline, one arc to follow. This myth of singularity is so deeply embedded in culture that questioning it often feels like questioning the rules of gravity. But what if the idea of "one life" is not a truth, but a program? What if your current path is only one possible expression of many that coexist in the background, waiting for a different signal from you?

There's a reason you sometimes feel like you're out of sync with your own life. Like something doesn't quite add up, even if everything looks fine on the surface. That dissonance isn't just personal dissatisfaction. It's the echo of a parallel script — a version of you that was never lived, but still pulses in your energetic field. You can feel it in moments of déjà vu, in those sudden longings that appear without logic, in the pull toward a version of yourself you've never been but somehow remember.

You've been trained to think linearly. You were told there's a beginning, a middle, and an end. But this is not how consciousness operates. Your mind is non-linear. So is time, once you remove the illusion created by clocks and calendars. In truth, there are many versions of you already written in potential. They are not fantasy. They are dormant scripts encoded in your field, each one waiting for activation. And each version of you exists with its own set of choices, patterns, relationships, and even emotional landscapes.

What determines which one becomes active? Not fate. Not chance. But alignment. Your frequency — the emotional, mental, and behavioral signal you emit — acts like a selector. It tunes you into one script while tuning out others. If you keep repeating the same emotional cycles, you stay locked into the same script. But if you interrupt the loop, even slightly, you open a crack through which a different storyline can enter.

The shift doesn't require external permission. It doesn't begin with a big life change. It begins internally, when you stop identifying with the role you've been playing and start accessing the energy of the role that's been waiting. This isn't about faking a new identity. It's about re-entering a deeper layer of self that has always existed, just beneath the noise of conditioning.

This is why inner work is not just healing — it's portal-building. Every time you release an inherited belief, you collapse one timeline and give birth to another. Every time you refuse a script that was handed to you, you recover the ability to write your own. And sometimes, this shift is subtle. A small decision. A single moment of clarity. But the energetic consequences are massive. You jump tracks. You start remembering what was never taught.

The idea of one life, one purpose, one outcome — it's comforting because it gives certainty. But it's also a cage. It erases possibility. It silences the versions of you that exist beyond the acceptable narrative. Those versions don't need to be imagined. They are already alive in potential, stored as energetic patterns that you can feel, sense, and eventually live. But you must become attuned to them. You must be willing to step off the script you've inherited, even before you know what the next one will look like.

This stepping off requires the courage to sit with the unknown. Most people cling to their current script not because it's aligned, but because it's familiar. The predictability of pain can feel safer than the uncertainty of expansion. But scripts don't disappear just because they are denied. They persist beneath the surface, pulling at the edges of your awareness until you finally turn to face them.

When you feel like life is passing you by, it's often because you're still tuned to a script that no longer matches your inner frequency. It's not that life isn't working. It's that the version of life you're inhabiting is misaligned with who you've become. This is why disruption often precedes transformation. The collapse of identity, the death of old ambitions, the sudden shifts in relationships — these are signs that the current script is breaking down to make room for something more truthful.

The friction you feel isn't failure. It's feedback. It's your inner system letting you know that another timeline is close. But it can't be accessed until you shed what was never yours to carry. That includes roles you inherited, desires you absorbed from others, and limitations you agreed to without questioning. Once these distortions are released, you don't need to "create" a new version of yourself. You just tune into it. You start receiving instructions from a different layer of your own consciousness.

Parallel scripts are not a metaphor. They are real energetic tracks encoded within you. Each one is governed by different assumptions, different choices, and a different level of permission. You can't enter a higher script while still obeying the constraints of a lower one. This is why breakthroughs often feel like betrayal. You're not just leaving behind a version of your life — you're walking away from an entire identity that once gave you meaning. You've probably already experienced this in fragments. A conversation that changed your perspective permanently. A decision that seemed small at the time but rerouted everything. An inner shift that didn't make sense logically, but altered how reality responded to you. These are not accidents. They are reminders that your life isn't one continuous stream, but a series of script junctions, each offering you a new role in the unfolding story.

The idea that you have to discover your one "true" path is part of the control mechanism. It keeps you chasing clarity instead of living in alignment. Real clarity doesn't come from the mind's analysis. It emerges as a felt sense when you are finally on the right frequency. When you step into the correct script, everything around you recalibrates. You don't need to force it. You become the resonant source, and reality adjusts to match.

This also means that nothing is ever wasted. Even scripts you want to escape taught you how they operate. They trained your awareness. They helped you recognize the difference between artificial choice and true inner directive. And that awareness is your access key. The more you recognize the signs, the easier it becomes to shift. The old world becomes transparent. You stop falling for the same illusions.

You are not bound to one script. You never were. That idea was planted to keep you compliant, to make you easier to predict, to ensure you wouldn't stray from the approved narrative. But your existence is multi-threaded. You are capable of living multiple lifetimes in one body. You just have to claim the authority to do so. Once you do, the myth of one life dissolves. And with it, so does the illusion of your limits.

How Emotional States Anchor You into Lower Versions of You

Your emotional state is not just a passing mood. It's an access code. It determines which version of reality you can perceive, and which version of yourself becomes active. Most people don't realize that when they feel stuck, overwhelmed, anxious, or numb, they aren't just experiencing emotions. They're sitting inside a frequency cage that limits the choices they can even see. These emotions anchor them to a specific version of their identity, a narrower version that feels familiar — even if it's painful.

Emotions act as stabilizers for your internal scripts. If a script is a sequence of thought, emotion, action, and outcome, then the emotional layer is the glue. When a certain emotional tone repeats — frustration, disappointment, helplessness — it doesn't just affect how you feel in the moment. It begins to fix your point of view into a specific storyline. That storyline will have specific thoughts attached to it. Specific behaviors. Specific outcomes. You're not reacting to life neutrally. You're reacting as the version of you that matches that emotional frequency.

That's why some people repeat the same patterns in different contexts — different job, different relationship, different city — but the same emotional cycles show up. The surface has changed, but the anchor point hasn't. Until that emotional anchor is identified and shifted, they will keep attracting and interpreting reality in the same way. They may even be shown opportunities for change, but they won't register them clearly. Or they'll dismiss them. Or they'll sabotage them. Not because they don't want change, but because they're not tuned to the version of themselves that can allow it.

This is where the concept of energetic anchoring becomes critical. Every emotional state corresponds to a specific energetic density. The heavier the emotion — guilt, shame, resentment — the tighter the tether to old scripts. These states create internal gravity. You become emotionally bound to an identity that cannot evolve. Not because you lack capability, but because you're orbiting the wrong emotional core.

Most people are trained to suppress, analyze, or bypass their emotions. But very few are taught to **observe the anchoring mechanism**. This means watching not only what emotion arises, but what *version of you* it activates.

Ask yourself: who am I when I feel this? What choices do I tend to make when I'm in this state? What thoughts become dominant? What beliefs suddenly feel true?

You'll notice that certain emotional states come with predictable inner scripts. Anger might trigger the version of you who always has to defend. Anxiety might activate the part of you who assumes something will go wrong. Shame might pull up the identity that constantly apologizes for existing. These emotional anchors are not flaws. They are learned adaptations, encoded through repetition and reinforced by past experiences. But once you become conscious of the sequence, you can begin to interrupt it.

This is where the shift starts. You don't need to force yourself into positive emotion. That rarely works. Instead, you bring full awareness to the emotion you're in and trace its code. You recognize the doorway it opens — or the trap it builds. And in that moment of recognition, you're no longer fused to it. You become the observer instead of the reactor.

The key to emotional unanchoring is not suppression, reactivity, or escape. It's mapping. If you can see the structure of the emotional state — where it begins, what it activates, what version of you emerges — you gain the power to make deliberate shifts. You're no longer bound to ride the same energetic script from trigger to action to outcome. Instead, you create an internal gap, a space where choice can exist.

This space is subtle but powerful. It doesn't scream. It whispers. It shows up as the moment where you feel yourself clench, tighten, brace. And then, instead of obeying the script that follows — the familiar reaction, the thought loop, the coping behavior — you pause and observe.

To support this, here's a tool you can use right now.

The Anchoring Awareness Tool

Use this in the moment or during reflective journaling. Its purpose is to reveal the pattern beneath your emotional states and to name the identity that each emotion activates.

1. **Name the Emotional State.** Not in general terms. Be precise. Is it irritation, disappointment, dread, guilt, jealousy, helplessness? Labeling with accuracy increases your clarity.

2. **Observe the Physical Signal.** Where do you feel it in your body? Throat tightness? Solar plexus contraction? Pressure in the chest? This is where the emotional frequency is being stored and repeated. These bodily signals are often the earliest signs of anchoring.

3. **Identify the Scripted Identity.** Ask: When I feel this way, who do I become? Do I shrink, defend, blame, chase, hide, perform, numb? Try to write it in a sentence: "When I feel [emotion], I become the one who _____."

4. **Track the Impulse.** What do you want to do next? Scroll, argue, eat, disappear, prove something, overachieve? This is the part of the script that's preparing to run. The urge itself is not a problem. But it's not the solution either. It's part of the loop.

5. **Ask the Disruptive Question.** "Is this who I choose to be?" Not from guilt. From power. You're not shaming the emotion. You're simply checking whether the identity it activates is aligned with the reality you want to create.

This tool creates the pause that rewrites the path. It doesn't demand that you feel differently. It invites you to stay conscious while feeling what you feel — and to step into authorship over how you relate to it.

Over time, you'll notice that many of your go-to emotional anchors are not current. They're echoes. They were formed during earlier moments in life, when you didn't have the tools to process or understand what was happening. The emotion became the holding pattern, the inner gravity. And from that emotional state, an identity formed. That identity became the one who coped. The one who survived. The one who made sense of the chaos. But that version of you is no longer the only one available.

You are not required to keep rehearsing pain just because it feels familiar. You are not bound to lower states just because they are energetically dense. The more you notice, the more you dissolve the automatic nature of emotional anchoring. And in that awareness, new versions of you begin to emerge — not by force, but by resonance.

The version of you that feels light, clear, sovereign, and rooted in truth is not a fantasy. It's a frequency. And like any frequency, it becomes more available the moment you disidentify from the patterns that once defined you.

This is not emotional bypassing. It's energetic precision. You're not escaping pain. You're choosing not to reenact it as your only available role. The script is not written in stone. It's written in state. And state can shift.

Let this tool become a daily practice. Use it to reclaim access to your full self. The one that is no longer defined by emotional gravity, but by the conscious energy you choose to hold.

Jump Protocols: The Real Technique Behind 'Quantum Shifting'

Most people hear "quantum shifting" and imagine it as some instant magical leap into a new life — a flick of mental intention that bends reality in a blink. The fantasy sounds good. But the real mechanics of shifting into a different timeline or identity are far more grounded, and much more powerful than vague visualizations or affirmations.

A true shift happens when the dominant frequency you emit becomes incompatible with the old version of your life. It's not about wishing your way out of a situation. It's about calibrating your internal state so consistently that reality has no choice but to respond. Not because you manipulated something externally, but because your internal signal became a new command line — one that the field around you can't ignore.

That's what this chapter is about: the practical, daily protocol for how to trigger that internal leap. Not in theory, but in energetic architecture.

Let's begin by dismantling the illusion.

There is no single event that causes a shift. Shifts are accumulated. They are made of invisible repetition — of moments when you choose the new frequency instead of recycling the old one. Each time you make that choice, you're not just thinking positively. You're rewriting the energetic script that tells reality who you are.

If you want to leave behind an identity, you have to stop speaking its language. That means interrupting the emotional patterns, behaviors, thoughts, and micro-decisions that feed it. That's the part no one teaches when they sell the shiny version of manifestation. But it's the part that matters.

Shifting doesn't happen when you say you're ready. It happens when you stop reactivating the conditions of the version you say you're leaving.

And this isn't about perfection. You don't need to be a flawless, vibrating saint to shift timelines. You only need to become intolerant of the vibrational residue that no longer belongs to the version you are choosing.

So how do you do that, practically?

You build a protocol. A system of deliberate anchors that stabilize the frequency of the version you're stepping into. Without this, most people simply snap back into the gravitational pull of their previous self. That's why they experience temporary highs, short bursts of clarity, or random manifestations — but then collapse back into old patterns.

The brain and body are wired for familiarity. Your nervous system has a memory. If you don't install a new default through intentional repetition, the pull of the old timeline will always win.

This is where the jump protocol comes in. It's a daily system designed not to convince you of your new identity, but to *experience* it so fully that the rest of your being begins to adapt. You don't become the new version through thought alone. You become it through full sensory saturation — through movement, feeling, choice, and presence.

Before breaking down the actual steps, you must internalize this: jumping is not teleportation. It is vibrational replacement. You are not running away from who you were. You are introducing a more powerful signal that gradually makes the old one irrelevant.

The more consistently you do this, the faster the external field will recalibrate around your new baseline. Results will follow, but the shift happens before the evidence. That's why most people sabotage the jump — they're waiting for proof before embodying the signal.

But the only proof you'll ever need is how your body feels when you're fully aligned with the version of you that already exists beyond this script.

Let's now move into the daily jump protocol itself. You'll be applying this not as a ritual of hope, but as a deliberate override. Each part of this sequence is a command to reality. Each step is an energetic pivot point.

1. The Signal Lock-In

Start the day with a frequency check. Not a to-do list, not a mental rehearsal of what must happen, but a direct tuning into the emotional and energetic signature of the identity you're choosing. Ask yourself, "What is this version of me tuned into right now?" Not what they *think*. What they *feel*. Where their attention is. What they care about. Then find it in your body.

This is not about imagination. It's about resonance. If you can't feel it, you haven't locked in. Stay with it. Use breath. Use music. Use stillness. Whatever tool brings the signal online, use it. This becomes the anchor of your day.

2. Pattern Interruption Through Physical Override

Throughout the day, the gravitational pull of the old identity will show up. Not always through obvious emotional reactions, but often through subtle micro-signals: tension, hesitation, irritability, procrastination, disassociation. These are not random. They are your nervous system returning to its old map.

When this happens, do not analyze. Do not justify. Override.

Override means doing something completely different with your *body*. Stand up. Shake it off. Speak a different sentence out loud. Interrupt the loop before it grows roots. The earlier you disrupt it, the less energy it drains and the faster your system adapts to the new version.

3. Micro-Decisions as Frequency Activators

You do not shift timelines by making one dramatic decision. You shift through the accumulation of small ones. The way you sit. The words you choose. The thing you delay or commit to. All these are coded with the identity you're in.

Start watching for these micro-decisions and use them to stabilize the jump. Each time you choose as the new version of you, you are programming a new script into the subconscious. This becomes the dominant code your life begins to run on.

4. Dismantle "Proof Addiction"

This is one of the biggest reasons jumps collapse. You start tuning into the new frequency, feeling aligned, acting in integrity with it, and then… nothing seems to happen. So you doubt. You look around. You look for proof. And the moment you do, you reenter the script of the old identity — the one that needs evidence before believing.

This addiction to proof is a parasite on your energetic field. Cut it.

Your reality is always delayed feedback. Your job is not to stare at the mirror, waiting for your reflection to smile first. Your job is to become the thing long enough that the field reshapes itself *because* it has no other option. That's how reality works.

5. Jump Sealing at Night

End the day with a conscious energetic closure. Not a review of what went wrong. Not a spiral of self-correction. But a declaration of alignment.

Ask: "Did I hold the signal longer than I used to?" Even one more moment than yesterday is a success. This is not about intensity, it's about duration. The longer you hold, the deeper the nervous system resets.

Seal the jump by connecting back to the signal of the identity you are moving into. Let it flood your system as you fall asleep. Let your dreams begin to build from that place. The subconscious is most malleable during the transition into sleep — use it.

Over time, this protocol rewires what your system considers normal. The jump is no longer a leap. It becomes your baseline. And from that baseline, new scripts, new outcomes, and new timelines begin to appear. Not because you forced them, but because you no longer emit the frequency that kept you trapped.

What you emit is what you access. The field doesn't care what you want. It responds to what you broadcast. This protocol is your method of transmission. Use it until the jump is no longer something you do — it's something you *are*.

Chapter 6. Language as Spell: How Words Lock You Into the Game

Why Most Self-Talk Reinforces the Loop

Most people don't realize that their inner dialogue is not neutral. The words you speak to yourself are not just observations or harmless expressions of how you feel. They are commands. And if you're not aware of the language you use, you might be reinforcing the very identity you're trying to escape.

Self-talk is one of the most underestimated forces in reality creation. It doesn't just describe your world. It builds it. Each time you repeat a sentence in your mind, each time you narrate your experience with familiar phrases, you are embedding another strand into the script that governs your perception, emotion, behavior, and results. If that language is patterned from an outdated identity, it does not free you. It traps you.

Most inner dialogue is unconscious repetition. It's filled with scripts inherited from caregivers, school systems, peer environments, media archetypes. You were not born thinking in loops like "I always mess this up" or "I'm not that type of person." These lines were absorbed. But they are sticky. They attach themselves to your internal voice and replay themselves whenever your system feels threatened, uncertain, or off-center.

This is where the problem begins. Because self-talk happens so quickly and so automatically, it bypasses conscious scrutiny. You might be actively doing the work of change on one level — choosing new behaviors, reading new material, even practicing new habits — but if your inner commentary is still coded in scarcity, shame, or helplessness, it cancels the shift. Your nervous system believes what your words repeat.

The power of self-talk lies in its frequency. The words you say to yourself are not one-off remarks. They are mantras, often repeated dozens or hundreds of times per day. And the subconscious doesn't care if you meant it as a joke, or if it slipped out because you were tired. It hears it. It records it. It treats it as data for how to keep you safe and consistent.

This is why affirmations don't work for most people. If the affirmation sits on top of a script that directly contradicts it, the subconscious doesn't buy in. Saying "I am worthy" once a day does not override the thousand micro-statements you make to yourself that suggest otherwise. Even worse, those positive phrases can activate resistance when the underlying script is unresolved. The mind responds with cynicism, detachment, or emotional shutdown. You feel like a fraud. Not because you are one, but because the inner voice has not been rewired.

To break this loop, you must stop seeing self-talk as a reaction and start treating it as a tool. You cannot wait for your emotional state to change before you change your language. You change your language *to shift* your state. The voice in your head has to be trained. Left alone, it will default to what it has always known.

But here's the subtle trap: not all negative self-talk is obviously negative. Some of the most damaging patterns hide under the appearance of logic, realism, or humility. Sentences like:

- "I'm just being honest with myself"
- "That's not really my strength"
- "This always happens to me"
- "I should be further by now"

These sound reasonable. They even feel responsible. But what they are really doing is cementing your past into your present. They are looping your previous limitations into today's identity, ensuring that tomorrow will repeat the same shape. This is not realism. This is quiet sabotage.

To shift this, you need to go beyond surface-level replacement of words. You need to *audit* the architecture of your inner language. Not just the overtly harsh lines, but the subtle phrases that operate like background code — unexamined, automatic, and powerful.

Let's now break that audit into a practical framework.

The Language Audit Exercise

To free yourself from these silent reinforcements, you must interrupt the default setting. The goal is not to immediately adopt perfect language. It's to bring precision and awareness to what has been operating without question.

Start by catching your automatic phrases in motion. Choose a single day to observe your self-talk. Not in a forced way, but with alert neutrality. Notice

the tone, the words, the repeated phrases that seem to come out without effort. Pay attention especially when you:
- Make a mistake
- Experience a delay or block
- Compare yourself to someone else
- Are asked to step into a larger version of yourself
- Reflect on your progress or lack of it

These moments are doorways. Your real script will reveal itself here. Often, it will come dressed as habit. "Of course this happened." "Why do I even try?" "I'm not built for that." These sentences might feel like passing thoughts. But they are not random. They are part of a system. And systems only change when the code is made visible.

Once you identify a recurring phrase, freeze it. Write it down, word for word, without softening it. Then ask yourself three specific questions:

1. **Whose voice is this originally?**
   Trace the pattern. Does it echo a parent, a teacher, a peer group, a cultural belief? The origin helps you recognize it's not truth. It's conditioning.

2. **What outcome does this phrase keep me tied to?**
   Be honest. If you keep saying this to yourself, what result does it lock in? What decisions do you avoid or delay because of it? What identity does it reinforce?

3. **What would a higher version of me say instead?**
   Don't just flip the sentence into a positive affirmation. Instead, craft a phrase that feels both aspirational and believable. Something your nervous system doesn't reject. Something your cells can begin to accept as possible.

You are not trying to sound motivational. You are rewriting internal code in a way that sticks. It must land in your body, not just your mind. A real language shift feels like truth returning to its original frequency. It sounds familiar, even if you've never spoken it aloud before.

Here's an example. Let's say the original phrase is: "I always fall back into my old habits." You trace it back to a dynamic of failure-rehearsal you absorbed growing up. You realize it makes you delay action, stay small, avoid trying again. Instead of forcing "I never fall back," which feels fake, you write: "Every time I notice the old pattern, I choose one different action." This is practical, grounded, and makes space for transformation without pressure.

When practiced consistently, this exercise creates micro-tears in the loop. The old script loses its emotional charge. The new phrasing builds muscle. Not all at once, but steadily. Your inner voice becomes less of an enemy and more of an ally. It stops anchoring you to the past and begins to assist your shift into a more congruent version of self.

The audit is not a one-time tool. It is ongoing. Even when you think the work is done, the script finds new ways to hide. It shows up in sarcasm, in delay language, in mock-humility. That's why this is not about controlling every word but about sharpening your *awareness* of the patterns that run beneath them.

Once your inner language stops colluding with your limitations, the rest of the system can follow. Thought, emotion, action, and outcome begin to realign. The loop loosens. New directions open. And what once felt like a battle with yourself becomes a quiet return to authorship. The voice in your mind is no longer just an echo. It becomes a tool of precision. A key. A compass. A code that finally serves *you*.

Decoder Protocol: Breaking the Verbal Patterns That Bind You

Words do not simply describe your reality. They structure it. And when you repeat certain verbal patterns long enough, they stop functioning as descriptions and start acting as permissions, permissions that bind you to invisible boundaries. These boundaries may sound like casual phrases or harmless self-commentary, but beneath them is code. Language is a carrier of your subconscious agreements.

You might think you're just venting when you say, "I'm always the one who gets overlooked," or "I just don't have the energy like other people." But those phrases are more than opinion. They are scripts encoded with identity anchors. The more you say them, the more you animate the version of yourself they describe.

This is how verbal patterning becomes binding: the structure of your words sets the range of your behavior. And the more your nervous system recognizes those structures, the more they become encoded into how you *feel*, not just what you *say*.

Most people believe that shifting behavior starts with changing actions. But you can try to act differently while still carrying the same verbal code. And the moment stress hits, you collapse back into the identity your language has rehearsed.

The only way to disrupt this cycle is through *precision decoding*. You don't just listen to your self-talk. You begin to study it. You dissect the phrasing that holds your identity together. And then you reconstruct it deliberately, in ways that allow new behavior, new decisions, new responses to emerge.

This is the foundation of the Decoder Protocol.

It begins by identifying the phrasing structures that operate like internal fences. These are rarely dramatic. They're usually subtle, disguised as personality traits or rational observations.

For example:
- "I've always been the kind of person who…"
- "That's just how I am."
- "I'm not the type who can…"
- "I don't do well with…"

Each of these is a linguistic loop. It holds in place a version of you that may no longer be accurate but still governs your options. These sentences are not just commentary. They are operating code. And like any code, they can be rewritten.

To do this, you need to isolate the recurring sentence structures you use to describe yourself, especially during tension or challenge. Notice not just *what* you say, but *how* you say it. Pay attention to the format, the phrasing, the rhythm. Repetition is the giveaway. Your subconscious always favors efficiency, so it will reuse the same constructions again and again.

Once you catch one, pause. The goal isn't to shame it or immediately force it to change. The goal is to pull it into view with neutrality and precision.

You then extract the internal logic. Ask yourself: If I say this repeatedly, what version of me is being stabilized? What expectations are baked into this sentence? What outcomes is it quietly shaping?

For example, a phrase like "I've always had trouble focusing" doesn't just describe a past experience. It contains three silent instructions: 1) expect difficulty, 2) avoid tasks that require deep attention, and 3) interpret future distraction as confirmation of the self-image.

Once you understand that, you gain access to the script beneath the phrase. And once you see the script, you can edit it.

But editing doesn't mean turning the phrase into empty positivity. The nervous system doesn't trust lies. If you replace "I've always had trouble focusing" with "I'm incredibly focused every day," your mind may reject it outright. The key is to find a rewrite that preserves truth while creating expansion. One that feels like a stretch, not a performance.

We'll now go deeper into exactly how to construct that new language. There is a formula that works, and when used consistently, it begins to rewire the way you speak, perceive, and respond.

Recode Language Script

The mind resists changes that feel fake. But it adapts rapidly to changes that feel precise, even if they stretch comfort. The goal of this protocol is not to manufacture surface positivity, but to build a new linguistic structure that your nervous system can actually trust. One that opens space instead of reinforcing limits.

To begin recoding a verbal loop, use this 3-part framework. Say the phrase aloud or write it out as you go:

1. **Acknowledge the pattern honestly.**
   Avoid pretending the loop never existed. You must name what was being reinforced. This gives your mind closure and signals that the old phrase no longer defines you.

2. **Interrupt the certainty.**
   Use flexible language that creates space for change. This step breaks the absolute structure that made the phrase rigid and binding.

3. **Insert new, expansive direction.**
   Not generic optimism. Use specific wording that suggests growth, possibility, or evolution that feels aligned with your current edge.

Here's how the transformation might look in practice:
Original loop:
"I've always had trouble focusing."

Step 1 – Acknowledge:
"I used to find it difficult to sustain focus, especially when overwhelmed."
Step 2 – Interrupt:
"But I've started noticing that it's not who I am, it's how I've been responding."
Step 3 – Insert expansion:
"More and more, I'm training my system to focus in shorter bursts with full presence."

This isn't about tricking yourself. It's about updating your internal language to reflect what's actually *possible* instead of what's been rehearsed. These new phrases operate as invitations, not declarations. You're not claiming a fake identity. You're installing linguistic scaffolding that allows a new version of you to take shape.

Once you write or speak your rewritten script, *pause*. Let it land in your body. Notice how it feels. If it generates a quiet sense of possibility or calm expectancy, you're on the right track. If it creates resistance or tension, it may still be too extreme or ungrounded in your current experience. Adjust the language until it feels honest, expansive, and doable.

This process isn't a one-time fix. Verbal patterns are built through repetition, and they're undone the same way. Each time you catch the old loop, you intervene and re-script. Eventually, the nervous system begins to expect the new phrasing. Your body becomes familiar with that version of expression, and behavior follows.

The real power lies in how quickly this shifts perception. Language isn't just how you describe your reality. It's how you filter what options even *exist* inside that reality. When your spoken words allow for more movement, your actual life begins to unfold with more freedom.

You'll also start noticing these patterns in others. Friends, family, colleagues—people narrate their own limitations constantly. You'll hear it everywhere. But instead of judging it, use it as confirmation: the world is built on linguistic loops, and those who master the script master the experience.

By recoding your language at the root, you are not "motivating" yourself. You are issuing new commands to your system. Subtle. Repetitive. Directed. With time, these shifts compound. You begin to speak differently, yes—but you also *listen* differently. You notice nuance, contradiction, opportunity. You become more sensitive to how words are programming not just thought, but identity itself.

This is what real rewiring looks like. Not just positive thinking, but script editing. Not just new habits, but new syntax. The Decoder Protocol gives you tools, but it also gives you sovereignty. Because once you recognize the verbal patterns that bound you, and rewrite them consciously, you are no longer just the character. You're the author. And the script begins to obey.

Script Glyphs: Power Words that Collapse Old Timelines

Language is not only a description of reality, but a spell cast upon it. Certain words carry more than meaning. They carry *charge*. They disrupt internal momentum and override neural loops. These are not simply affirmations or intentions. They are what this protocol calls **Script Glyphs**—encoded words that act as keys, collapsing the weight of timelines that no longer serve your trajectory.

A Script Glyph is not just a powerful word. It's a trigger word encoded with frequency and identity. It is spoken not to explain, but to shift. When a glyph is spoken with full internal coherence, it pierces through the auto-narration of your life and introduces a rupture point. The old timeline hesitates. And in that hesitation, choice returns.

You have already felt this, even if unconsciously. A word like *enough* spoken with clarity at the end of a toxic cycle. A word like *return* whispered in the middle of grief. Or *initiate* used at the edge of transformation. These words don't just convey emotion. They collapse cluttered momentum. They are compact carriers of command.

Most people, however, use language as commentary. The words they speak mirror the current state rather than shaping the next one. This is because their words emerge from identity loops, not from inner authority. To shift your timeline, your language must operate as an *override*, not a reaction. That's where glyphs come in.

Glyphs don't need to be long or poetic. In fact, the simpler they are, the more directly they bypass mental filters. The effectiveness comes from the context, the internal state, and the deliberate energetic delivery. When you speak a glyph, you're not trying to convince yourself. You are issuing a non-negotiable instruction to the energetic field around and within you.

This requires presence. Speaking without internal alignment weakens the glyph. You cannot collapse timelines with performative declarations. The words must come from what is real. Real pain. Real readiness. Real command.

The spoken glyph is most effective when it follows a moment of deep recognition. For example, after catching yourself in a thought loop, a glyph can finalize the break. Or after realizing an inherited pattern, a glyph can mark the refusal. In that sense, glyphs are like energetic closures. They seal what no longer belongs and open what is newly available.

Let's make this practical.

Imagine you've just recognized an internal narrative that has kept you seeking approval. You see how often you shape your words to fit others' expectations. You feel it in the body. The ache in the throat. The subtle anxiety before speaking.

At that exact moment—when recognition is fresh and the emotional loop is vulnerable—you speak:

"Return."

The glyph signals a collapse of external orientation. You are calling yourself back to center. Not just saying it, but doing it. The word is not for the mind. It is for the field. You speak it once, clearly, with breath behind it. And then you let the shift settle.

Not every word will be your glyph. That's why this is not a memorization game. Glyphs are discovered, not assigned. They arise through experience and clarity. Some may stay with you for years. Others may arrive only for a specific cycle. But each one, when used consciously, becomes a collapse point for scripts you no longer choose to carry.

To activate a glyph, the words alone are not enough. What makes them collapse old timelines is not their surface meaning, but the inner voltage behind them. Each glyph must be treated as a loaded signal, not a sentence. You are not trying to change your mindset. You are issuing a directive to your reality structure. This requires silence, awareness, and then decisive release.

A glyph used too early, before the charge is present, does nothing. A glyph used too late, after the loop has re-solidified, gets absorbed as more noise. The key is *timing*. You speak the glyph in the gap—the precise space when a pattern is cracking, and before a new loop forms. That's when the structure is soft enough to reconfigure.

This is not for theatrics. You are not yelling into the void. You are transmitting code into the subtle layers of your script. That is why the moment must be real. You cannot fake clarity. You wait for it. You feel it. You know when the timeline is about to loop again. That's the entry point. Let's move into practice.

Glyph Activation Tool

This protocol is designed to help you identify, charge, and activate Script Glyphs. Do not rush through it. If done correctly, it will function as a reset mechanism, not just a mindset tweak.

1. Catch the Fracture Point

This is the precise moment where you recognize the old loop returning. It could be a familiar self-judgment, a reactive pattern, or a compulsive thought track. Pause everything. Do not analyze. Just stop. You're holding the doorway open.

2. Feel the Charge

Don't run from the emotion. The power of a glyph comes from the charge behind it. Let the discomfort build without labeling it. Is it shame? Fear? Pressure? Let the body speak. The more raw it feels, the more potent the shift will be.

3. Listen for the Glyph

Now listen. Not with the mind. With your field. A word will emerge. It might be one you've heard before, or it might be new. Trust what arises. You're not inventing a mantra. You're retrieving a code.

Some common glyphs include:
Break.
Return.
Now.
Exit.
Seal.
Shift.
Cut.
Here.
No.
Undo.
Root.
Null.

But none of these will work unless they match your moment. If nothing arises, wait longer. This is not a linguistic exercise. It's a recognition.

4. Speak it Once

When you find it, speak it. Once. Clearly. Out loud if possible. Do not explain it. Do not soften it. The glyph is not asking for permission. It is delivering a verdict. The tone should be clear, calm, but final. The moment you speak it, *stop*. Let the shift ripple. Don't add commentary.

5. Observe the Collapse

What thoughts try to return? What emotional echoes try to restabilize the loop? Do nothing. Simply observe. The glyph has already been spoken. You are not reinforcing the old structure by wrestling it. Let it decompose.

6. Anchor the New Baseline

After the collapse, you may feel space, silence, or an unfamiliar stillness. This is good. This is the space you once filled with auto-looping thought. Do not rush to fill it. Just stay there. Let your nervous system recalibrate to the absence of noise. This is where the new script writes itself.

7. Repeat Only When Real

Glyphs do not need repetition to work. They need sincerity. You may use the same glyph again, but only if the moment is new. Never turn your glyph into a habit phrase. The more charged and precise the use, the more power it holds.

This tool is not for casual affirmation. It is for timeline interference. The moment you speak a glyph from full awareness, the energetic trajectory shifts. The future that was being constructed collapses, and another becomes accessible. You don't have to know what it is yet. You just made it possible.

Let this tool become part of your reality editing process. The more fluently you listen, the more precisely you will speak. In the silent space between loops, you will no longer echo the past. You will write your next signal from origin, not repetition.

That is the essence of a glyph. One word. Fully chosen. Spoken with authority. And everything shifts.

Part III. Accessing the Rewrite Layer

You've seen the code. You've felt it move beneath your thoughts, your habits, your choices. You've traced the loops, exposed the layers, and begun to interrupt the momentum of the false. That work was not preparation. It *was* the work. But now comes the inflection point—the part most never reach.

To rewrite reality, you must move from disruption into authorship. Not of fantasy, but of internal precision. This is not about imagining a better version of yourself. It's about *switching to the layer* where those versions already exist, and choosing the one that aligns with your signal.

There is a point in the system where old scripts cannot follow. A deeper current where mental noise thins out, and the pattern stops repeating itself. Most people never access this space because they are still busy trying to fix the noise. They're still arguing with their old programming, trying to correct it with nicer words, better behavior, or longer meditations.

But correction is not creation. And control is not authorship.

What this next part of the journey requires is not more effort, but more *exactness*. You must enter the layer where language becomes architecture. Where thought stops being internal commentary and becomes external design. Where perception becomes a scalpel, not a mirror.

This is the rewrite layer. Not a metaphor, not a technique—an actual energetic and neurological state. It is quiet. It is sober. It is sharp. When you enter it, you don't feel euphoric. You feel awake. You stop asking the same questions. You stop defending your limitations. You stop seeking permission to move.

Here, you don't need to prove your value. You choose your vector. You don't ask who you are. You speak from the place that knows. And you don't get there by believing harder—you get there by letting go of every signal that never belonged to you.

Part 3 is not about healing the old timeline. It's about building the new one while the old one dissolves behind you. You'll learn how to run new identity sequences without contradiction, access states that collapse multiple timelines at once, and install new core scripts from stillness, not strain.

This is the layer where real influence begins. Where the words you speak are not wishes but signals. Where energy is not something you try to raise—it's something you transmit with precision. Where reality is not something that happens to you, but something that calibrates around your chosen frequency.

You are not chasing transformation. You are wielding it.

And you are no longer asking the loop to set you free.

You are walking straight out of it.

Chapter 7. Stillness as Access: Entering the Rewrite Zone

Why Action Alone Can't Change the Script

In every self-help formula, action is the golden idol. Act more. Try harder. Push through. Discipline yourself into a new outcome. And for a while, it seems to work. You build new habits, follow the plan, do the steps. But something doesn't quite shift. The surface changes, but the weight underneath stays the same. Your reality bends slightly, then snaps back to where it began.

That's because action without access to the underlying script is cosmetic. It rearranges the furniture in a house that's built on a faulty blueprint. The structure may look different, but it still functions according to the same invisible pattern.

The script is what makes certain actions feel impossible and others inevitable. It is the layer that assigns meaning before your mind even catches up. You are not just doing things—you are *acting from* something. If that something remains intact, your action becomes a loop disguised as movement.

Every action you take is executed from a particular identity. And every identity is running on a belief matrix, mostly unspoken and unexamined. If you haven't altered that identity, the action you take will be filtered through its limitations.

You can start a business, but if the internal directive is "I'm not the kind of person who succeeds," the business will shape itself around that narrative. You'll attract friction where there should be flow. You'll self-correct in the direction of your subconscious belief, even while your conscious mind insists you want more.

This is why change often feels like sabotage. The moment you start building a new pattern, the old one reacts—not out of cruelty, but out of loyalty. The subconscious doesn't want what's exciting or transformative. It wants what's familiar. And when action contradicts familiarity, the system triggers friction.

The more disciplined your actions become, the more resistance you feel. Not because you're doing something wrong, but because the deeper layer hasn't been rewritten. You're forcing new code through an old channel, and the signal keeps getting distorted.

This is why motivation wears off. Why hustle leads to burnout. Why even the most intelligent strategies sometimes fail. Not because they're flawed, but because they are operating in a field shaped by a different instruction set. And unless you edit that set, every effort will be rerouted.

There's a reason why the same action works for one person and collapses for another. Two people can post the same content, launch the same product, speak the same words—and get entirely different results. The difference isn't the action. It's the frequency it's carried on. The belief it's plugged into. The identity it's anchored in.

Action is the outer signal. But the script is the transmitter. If you don't update the transmitter, the signal remains weak, scrambled, or misinterpreted by the field.

The system is far more sophisticated than we've been taught. It doesn't respond to effort. It responds to congruence. And congruence is impossible when your outer motion contradicts your inner command.

This is why some people can do very little and yet generate huge impact, while others do everything and see only small ripples. Reality is not rewarding motion. It is reflecting the precision of signal.

The subconscious does not listen to what you say. It listens to what you *run*. And if the program running underneath your action is built on fear, lack, or false loyalty to the past, the field will mirror that—not what you were hoping for.

We are not here to shame action. Action is sacred. But action only becomes powerful when it is executed from the correct layer. And that layer is not force, strategy, or discipline. It is identity.

Identity is the true command center. It defines what feels natural, what feels possible, and what feels like self-betrayal. When you attempt action that doesn't align with your encoded identity, you will feel inner resistance, not because you're lazy or unmotivated, but because you are violating an invisible rule you never consciously agreed to.

Most of the time, the script was written before you even had language to name it. It formed through emotion, repetition, tone of voice, early rewards and punishments. You were taught what you were, what you should want, how far you could go, and what happens when you reach too far. You didn't write these codes, but you inherited them. And now, every decision you make gets filtered through them unless they are consciously rewritten.

That's why so many people who do the "right" things still feel stuck. They're living from a script that contradicts their current desires. And no amount of hustle can override a deep internal command that says, "This isn't safe," or "This isn't you." The nervous system will interpret progress as danger, and it will push you back into the safety of the loop.

This is also why people return to toxic relationships, abandon healthy routines, or sabotage money just as it begins to flow. It's not that they want to fail. It's that success violates the old script's boundary conditions. And unless those are rewritten, the subconscious will always course-correct.

The paradox is that action is still required—but only after the inner script has shifted. When the rewrite is real, action becomes expression, not effort. You no longer have to force your way forward because you are acting from a self that has already integrated the new trajectory. The field feels it. So do the people around you. And most importantly, so does your own body.

The shift isn't in trying harder. It's in learning how to shift the place you're acting from. That begins by identifying what part of you is choosing the action. Is it the part of you that's still trying to be good enough? Still trying to compensate for old shame? Still trying to finally prove something to someone who's no longer watching? Or is it coming from the part of you that already knows who you are, even if the external reality hasn't yet caught up?

Until that distinction is made, the loop remains active. You'll change what you do but not who you are while doing it. You'll climb the mountain but feel like a fraud at the top. You'll win the prize and feel emptier than before. Because action disconnected from self creates progress that feels hollow.

When the script is updated, the external results often come faster—but not because you're "doing more." They come because the reality field responds to internal congruence. The actions land differently. The words carry a different frequency. You're not pretending. You're not performing. You're not hustling to outrun a shadow you never stopped to name. You are transmitting from the layer that creates.

In this space, you may still feel challenge, but it won't feel like sabotage. You may still face resistance, but it will no longer feel like confusion. You'll know the difference between the friction of expansion and the friction of dissonance. One invites you to grow. The other warns you that you are acting from an outdated signal.

The script doesn't change through motion alone. It changes when the motion arises from a self that has dissolved the lie and written something new in its place. From that moment on, every step you take begins to align. Not because you forced it to, but because you no longer needed to. You became the transmission. And reality simply listened.

Accessing the Silent Layer Between Thought and Form

There is a space within you that speaks no language, holds no opinion, and makes no effort to be seen. It is not your mind, your emotion, or your energy field, although all of these pass through it. It is what remains when none of those are trying to define your experience. And it is from this place that reality begins to take shape.

Most people live entirely above this layer, moving from one thought to another, reacting to sensations, interpreting feelings, chasing clarity through noise. Even when trying to "be present," the mind often clings to technique, to form, to analysis. But presence does not require effort. It requires subtraction. And the layer where subtraction becomes perception is the silent space before thought becomes form.

You've been conditioned to act quickly, speak decisively, and think in complete sentences. Yet most of what truly moves you arises before any of those mechanisms can label it. Before the thought of fear, there is a contraction. Before the desire, there is a pulse. Before the idea, there is a subtle vibration that moves toward creation. That is the layer you are learning to access.

This layer is not mystical in a removed or inaccessible sense. It is not something you earn, nor something only monks or mystics can reach. It is quite the opposite. It is the most natural, native layer of consciousness, and it is always active. What makes it feel distant is the constant noise layered on top of it.

To access this silent layer, you do not need hours of meditation, elaborate rituals, or altered states. You need stillness—not as the absence of movement, but as the absence of interference. And the most powerful entry point is what we'll call *micro-stillness*.

The Micro-Stillness Method

Micro-stillness is the practice of entering the silent layer by pausing before the thought fully forms. It is the moment just before reaction, the inhale before speech, the instant before decision. These are windows. And they are always available, no matter what your external environment looks like.

The method begins with noticing. You don't try to force silence. You simply watch the space between stimuli and response. When someone speaks, wait before responding. When a desire arises, pause before labeling it. When an idea forms, hold it for a beat before following it. In that space, something else becomes available—a perception not filtered through programming.

Start small. You might begin by applying micro-stillness to the first five minutes of your day. Instead of reaching for your phone, sit up slowly and listen. Feel what's present in your body without naming it. Let your thoughts come, but don't chase them. You're not trying to stop them, only to observe the gap between their appearance and your engagement.

This space can feel strange at first, even disorienting. That is because most of your life has trained you to fill space, not enter it. But the discomfort is not danger. It is unfamiliarity. And within that unfamiliarity is the doorway to the rewrite layer.

Thoughts lose some of their grip when you meet them from silence. They begin to dissolve instead of spiral. Emotions begin to process themselves rather than possess you. And the reality you perceive begins to stretch, as if time itself makes space for you to choose, rather than react.

This method is not about controlling your mind. It is about slipping underneath it. When practiced regularly, it starts to rewire your default frequency. You move from compulsive reaction to conscious creation. You begin to notice that before anything becomes real, it first becomes felt. And that feeling does not begin in the mind.

Once you begin to trust that layer, you'll notice something shift in how time operates. Moments expand. Choices feel less rushed. It's not because you're thinking slower, but because you're no longer held hostage by the mind's urgency. Thought still arrives, but you no longer mistake it for truth. You see it as one of many possible scripts forming at the edge of perception.

Micro-stillness strengthens the muscles of discernment. It is in that half-second pause that you can ask the quiet question, "Is this mine?" Is the emotion moving through you the result of your own deeper sensing, or a program triggered by a cue? Is the action you're about to take a response aligned with your inner architecture, or a reflex anchored in the past? These questions are not always answered with language, but felt as clarity or dissonance in the body. The body speaks before the mind constructs reasons.

This layer also dissolves false urgency. So much of modern life is constructed to keep you in a loop of constant engagement. Notifications, deadlines, decisions, validation-seeking, productivity pressure—it's all scripted to prevent you from ever touching that quiet space. But the more you learn to move from the silent layer, the less you're seduced by urgency that isn't yours. You begin to detect the difference between motion and movement. Not everything that moves you forward is aligned. Some things just keep you spinning faster inside the same loop.

The silent layer is also where deeper intelligence speaks. Not the intellect that solves problems, but the intelligence that designs the game. This is where hunches emerge, visions arrive, and unexplainable clarity pierces through noise. You don't control when it happens, but you create the condition that makes it possible. Silence is that condition. And once you realize this intelligence doesn't shout, you begin to value quiet more than noise, stillness more than drama.

In moments of deep micro-stillness, the veil of mental narration fades. You may catch the impulse to speak about something that hasn't even happened yet and let it dissolve before it leaves your lips. You may feel an old emotion rise like a wave but no longer let it define the next hour of your life. The space between the stimulus and your identity starts to widen. And in that space, new versions of you begin to emerge—not forced, but allowed.

This work also builds subtle strength. It takes far more power to pause than to react. In the silent layer, you are not suppressing response, but owning it. You're stepping out of the automatic path long enough to question who built it. That is not weakness. That is sovereignty.

Eventually, this micro-stillness seeps into motion. You're walking, but you're aware of your steps. You're in conversation, but still rooted in presence. You're moving through the world, but not pulled by it. You're not trying to freeze life. You're slowing the mechanism that interprets it, and by doing so, you change what is possible within it.

It may not look dramatic to anyone else. But internally, the shifts are tectonic. You no longer identify with every thought. You no longer follow every emotional thread. You begin to shape your perception with precision. That's the foundation of real transformation.

The silent layer is not just a refuge. It's a control panel. Not in the mechanical sense, but as the place from which all perception can be altered. Every script is written from the energetic tone you hold in that layer. If you can sit with that tone before it becomes thought, if you can refine it, clarify it, or even empty it, then the reality that flows from it cannot help but shift. Micro-stillness is the door. What's behind it is not silence, but source. And the more often you enter, the less you live as a puppet of thought, and the more you become the author of it.

How to Use Micro-Stillness to Alter Outcomes in Real Time

You don't need hours of silence to change your life. You need seconds of precision. That's the hidden architecture of micro-stillness. It isn't a lifestyle—it's a tool. And when used correctly, it becomes a moment-by-moment lever of influence over your experience and the outcomes it produces.

Most people believe change happens after the fact. You reflect, you journal, you try to do better next time. But reality doesn't wait for your debrief. It molds itself in the now, reacting to the state you are in when a decision is made, when a word is spoken, when a subtle signal is sent into a room. This is where the power of real-time micro-stillness becomes visible. It lets you step into the very machinery of unfolding moments and recode them before they lock in.

The principle is simple: all outer outcomes are shaped by inner state. Your energy emits before your words do. Your presence lands before your behavior is registered. If the energy you carry is fragmented, reactive, or coded with unconscious beliefs, the reality that mirrors back to you will be shaped accordingly. Micro-stillness lets you interrupt that broadcast before it takes hold.

But this is not about stillness for its own sake. It's not about blankness. It's about recalibration. The goal is not to pause forever. The goal is to enter stillness just long enough to reset the signal you are sending into the field.

That field responds not to what you want but to what you are. Micro-stillness gives you access to what you are in the precise moment that matters most: the moment before engagement. That microsecond window—right before you reply, before you act, before you decide—is where the script either continues as written or gets rewritten by your awareness.

This is not meditation in the traditional sense. You don't need a mat. You don't need solitude. You don't even need silence around you. You need internal space. You could be in a meeting, in a heated conversation, in the middle of a task. The practice is invisible. That's what makes it powerful.

The Ritual of Real-Time Rewrite

This is where practice turns into protocol. The goal is not to stop everything you're doing but to drop into a brief still point within the activity. A pause that allows you to check your state, not in retrospect, but in the now.

You begin by cultivating micro-awareness of energetic shifts. These shifts are usually felt before they are noticed. You sense a tightening in your body, a rushing in your thoughts, a compulsion to defend or prove, a contraction in your presence. These are indicators that you are being pulled into a scripted loop. The signal is no longer coming from intention but from reaction. That's your cue.

When you catch that cue, you don't need to analyze it. You simply halt. Not externally, but internally. You bring your awareness back to the present moment by doing one thing: suspending interpretation.

This is the essence of real-time micro-stillness—suspending the mental narrative for just a few seconds. Not replacing it with a new thought, not affirming something better, not fixing anything. Just holding. Creating a space where no new words are formed. Where emotion is not judged. Where nothing is added.

From that stillness, clarity emerges.

Once the mind stops compulsively narrating and the body no longer grips the moment through unconscious tension, what's left is a neutral field. In that space, you're no longer reacting from memory or identity. You're not defending an old version of yourself. You're simply aware. And from awareness, you can insert a new signal. A subtle shift in posture, breath, tone, or presence that sends a different instruction to the moment.

You don't have to know exactly what to do next. You just need to stop letting the old script fill in the blanks for you. When you hold the still point long enough, the need to fill it with something fades. What arises instead is an intuitive impulse—clean, unforced, and aligned. This impulse is not rooted in performance or pressure. It's a movement from your center. And that movement is what begins to bend the outcome in a new direction.

Stillness disrupts the energy that would have otherwise driven a familiar result. The anger that would've erupted. The approval-seeking that would've distorted your words. The fear that would've made you smaller. All of it loses momentum. In its place, something rare appears: sovereignty in real time.

This is not about suppressing emotion. It's about interrupting the chain reaction that emotion usually triggers. You're not pushing anything down. You're letting it surface without letting it steer. That's the power of awareness without identification. You see the emotion. You feel the energy. But you don't hand it the microphone. You give it space to dissolve before it speaks for you.

There is a specific way to ground this in daily life, and it requires precision.

The Real-Time Rewrite Protocol

1. **Catch the Shift**

    Notice the moment your state changes. It could be subtle—tight shoulders, shallow breath, pressure in your chest. Don't analyze. Just mark it.

2. **Suspend the Feed**

    Stop interpreting the moment. No story, no evaluation, no reaction. Let the mental commentary freeze. One breath held in silent awareness is enough.

3. **Anchor into Sensation**

    Drop into the physical now. Feel your feet on the ground, the breath in your nose, the space behind your eyes. You're not escaping the moment. You're entering it with no filter.

4. **Let the Old Signal Die**

    Don't rush to fix or replace. Just hold. The emotional charge will try to reassert itself. Stay still. If necessary, soften your body. Soften your face. Stay empty.

5. **Send the New Signal**

    From the stillness, choose your next micro-move. This may be a shift in how you look at someone. It may be the delay before you speak. It may be the decision to walk away. Let it rise from alignment, not programming.

6. **Re-enter Clean**

    Come back into the moment, but do so as the version of you that chose, not the version that reacted. This locks in a different outcome, even if externally the moment looks similar.

With practice, this protocol becomes invisible. No one around you will notice what you're doing, but everything will start to feel different. Conversations soften. Opportunities appear. Resistance lessens. You're not changing others—you're interrupting the energetic patterns that used to dictate how moments played out. That alone reshapes the script.

And in that silence you've carved—seconds long, but infinite in power—you become the architect of reality. Not by force, not by effort, but by precision. That's the kind of control that can't be seen, only felt. That's real influence. And it begins the moment you stop participating in a reality you didn't choose.

Let others speak louder. Let others move faster. You'll move better. Because you know where the real power is.

In the stillness before the moment breaks.

Chapter 8. The True Mechanics of Manifestation
(and Why It's Not Working for You)

The Manifestation Lie: What You Were Never Told

Most people who feel stuck are not lacking ambition, clarity, or even energy. They're following a set of rules they were told would work—but were never designed to. Especially in the manifestation world.

The narrative is seductive: if you visualize hard enough, write affirmations daily, hold a positive state, and "believe," reality will shape itself around your intentions. And if it doesn't? You must not be aligned enough. You must be blocked. You must not want it deeply enough.

This is the loop that keeps people trapped—chasing their own shadows under the illusion of empowerment. Because here's the part no one tells you: most mainstream manifestation teachings are built on false assumptions about how reality actually forms. They treat your mind like a vending machine. Input a thought, wait for the output. Repeat until results arrive.

But your current life is not shaped by the thoughts you affirm. It's shaped by the unspoken script that runs underneath them.

You can say, "I am abundant" 500 times a day. But if your nervous system is wired to equate abundance with danger, loss, or abandonment, you won't move toward it—you'll subtly sabotage every attempt to receive it. And then you'll blame yourself for not "manifesting right."

The real mechanism behind reality-shaping is not linear. It is not thought leads to emotion, leads to action, leads to result. It's deeper and less visible. It begins in what we could call your *core identity field*—a subconscious blueprint made up of silent beliefs, stored memories, energetic imprints, and inherited patterns. This field emits a frequency long before you speak, act, or even think. That's what sets the stage for manifestation. Not what you want. Not what you say. But what your system has been coded to *expect*.

That expectation operates beneath awareness. It's what you prepare for without realizing it. It's the version of the world your body believes is "safe" to experience—even if it's painful. That's why so many people oscillate. They see a glimpse of possibility, feel hope, and begin to shift. Then an internal alarm gets triggered. Too good. Too different. Too much. The body reels it back. The old script reboots. And they call it sabotage.

But it's not sabotage. It's protection. The system is choosing the devil it knows over the unknown it secretly desires.

This is the hidden physics of manifestation. The outcome you receive is the one your identity can *hold*. Not momentarily. Not when you're in a high-vibe bubble. But consistently, from a regulated state, even when things feel uncertain. If your internal structure is still anchored to an identity of struggle, not enoughness, or unworthiness, you will magnetize what confirms that reality—regardless of what you say out loud.

This is why results often seem so random. Some people barely visualize or script, yet they seem to receive effortlessly. Others dedicate hours to rituals, vision boards, and affirmations but remain stuck. It's not a matter of discipline or desire. It's a matter of congruence between internal coding and external experience.

And that congruence cannot be faked.

You can't "think" your way into a different field. You can't trick the system by saying things you don't believe. The energetic field that manifests outcomes listens to the deepest layer of your system, not the surface one.

So the real question becomes: What version of you is doing the manifesting? Is it the one that was taught to prove, to earn, to chase love by becoming more? Is it the one performing the rituals because it's terrified of being left behind? Or is it the version of you that no longer needs the outcome to feel whole?

Until you collapse the performance layer—the part of you using "manifestation" to fix yourself—everything you try to create will be filtered through distortion.

This is where the lie hides: in the idea that reality will shift if you just say the right things in the right order with the right mindset.

The idea that your thoughts alone control outcomes is comforting because it feels actionable. You can visualize. You can write. You can repeat mantras. But the truth is, it's not the *content* of your thinking that shapes your world.

It's the *origin* of the thinking. Most people don't notice that their desire to manifest is rooted in a subconscious belief that something is missing. And when you reach for something from a place of lack, you don't draw it closer. You reinforce the distance.

That's the trap.

Wanting isn't wrong. Vision isn't wrong. But trying to bypass your internal wiring with external effort creates a frequency mismatch that stalls everything. You're essentially asking for a new life while holding the vibration of the old one. And that dissonance is what most people call "stuckness."

The system responds to coherence, not words. It listens to your actual relationship with self, not the language you layer on top of it. This is why someone with deep trust in their worth can receive things without asking. They don't need to command the universe. They're not trying to manipulate energy. They're simply aligned. Their nervous system isn't bracing for disappointment, so there's no friction in the field. The result becomes natural.

But when your self-talk is a performance, when it's used to compensate for something you haven't truly cleared, you're speaking in code the system doesn't trust. It detects the hesitation, the charge, the need beneath the affirmation. That charge carries a signal, and the signal gets honored. Every time.

This is where the manifestation narrative becomes not only misleading but damaging. Because it teaches people to fix the wrong layer. To tweak language. To polish intention. To double down on discipline. But it skips the root: the encoded identity that expects something different than what the mouth is saying.

And often, that identity was formed in survival.

You may have learned that asking leads to rejection, that visibility is unsafe, or that good things come with a cost. These impressions live deeper than thought. They live in the fascia, the breath, the way your body tightens when something good starts to happen. And until that level shifts, nothing sustainable can emerge.

So what works? Not more control. Not more effort. But more honesty.

When you tell the truth about what you're actually expecting—not what you wish to expect, but what your body *believes* will happen—you begin to surface the real program. And once it's seen, it can be recoded. But only if you stop trying to outrun it.

This is the paradox: you change your reality not by obsessively trying to shift it, but by learning to *stop broadcasting fear through the act of trying.*

Manifestation becomes natural when there's nothing in the system contradicting it. When the desire doesn't carry the charge of desperation. When the intention doesn't scream, "Please fix me." That's when the field opens.

It's not about becoming perfect. It's about becoming clear.

Clarity means you're no longer negotiating with your old story. You're not begging the universe to overwrite it. You're not reciting a script to convince yourself you're worthy. You're not swinging between hope and frustration, measuring your alignment by how quickly something arrives.

You're present, clean, still, and plugged into a deeper reality where you're not trying to get anything. You're remembering that you already are the version of you who belongs there.

The real lie of manifestation is that you have to fight for the life you want. The truth is, you only need to stop defending the one that no longer fits.

Energy Matching vs Forced Visualization

Most people were taught to visualize as a way to manifest. Close your eyes, imagine what you want, and try to feel like it's already yours. The theory makes sense: by aligning your thoughts and emotions with the desired outcome, you're supposed to draw it closer. But there's an unspoken flaw in this logic that very few recognize.

When you're *forcing* visualization, you're actually creating resistance.

The truth is, your system knows when you're pretending. If you're imagining something that your nervous system doesn't believe is possible, it creates an internal dissonance. You might try to see yourself with more money, with a different body, in a new relationship, but underneath, your body is tense, your breath is shallow, and a silent doubt is running like background noise. That signal—the real one—overrides the fantasy every time.

Visualization isn't supposed to be a performance. It's supposed to be an *emergence*. A natural byproduct of a state you already feel safe embodying. The more you try to force it, the more your system interprets it as something separate, something outside, something not yet safe or accessible. And that pushes it further out of reach.

Energy matching, on the other hand, bypasses this tension.

When you match the *frequency* of a reality, you don't need to see it perfectly. You don't even need to know exactly what it will look like. You're not rehearsing a movie scene in your head. You're aligning your internal state with the *qualities* of the version of you who already lives there.

This means tuning into ease before evidence. Trust before certainty. Expansion before logic. It's the difference between pretending to be rich in your head and embodying the energy of someone who no longer fears survival. That shift can't be faked. It has to be accessed through presence, not projection.

This is where people get stuck. They believe that because they can't see the outcome clearly, they're not manifesting correctly. But often, the more vivid the image, the more attached you become to controlling how it unfolds. And attachment always tightens the field. It creates tension. And tension signals mistrust.

Instead of building imaginary scenes, start attuning to the tone of the version of you who already feels it as done. Not from a mental concept, but from a felt internal register. What does their breath feel like? How do they walk into a room? How do they pause before answering a question? What don't they need to explain anymore?

Let that be the entry point.

And here's the part that's rarely taught: you can *only* hold that frequency consistently if your system believes it's safe to do so. If you haven't addressed the internal alarms that get triggered when things get good—if receiving still feels dangerous, unfamiliar, or undeserved—then you'll fall back into old loops, even if your visualization is flawless.

This is why energy matching is a deeper process than just sitting and thinking. It requires you to *feel safe in the reality you're calling in*, even if it's unfamiliar. That safety has to be built inside your body before it can stabilize in your life.

Start by removing the pressure to "see" anything. This is not about imagination. It's about sensation.

Sit or stand, but let your body settle. Breathe into the lower belly. Let the breath deepen without controlling it. Now, recall a moment—even a small one—when you felt naturally at ease. Not euphoric, not high, just calm. Maybe it was after a conversation that went better than expected. Or a morning when nothing felt rushed. Let your system remember that tone.

Now here is where the real shift happens: start layering onto that sense of ease the emotional signature of the version of you who already lives in the new timeline. Not what they have, not what they do. Just how they *feel*. Not hypothetically, but physically. Use sensation, not imagery.

Ask: if the version of me who already lives in alignment with this outcome were breathing through this body right now, how would they do it?

Let your breath shift. Let your posture adjust without forcing it. Notice if your shoulders need to drop. Notice the silence that comes when you stop trying to "achieve" and start letting something familiar emerge from underneath all the effort.

Then bring your attention to your chest. Soften there. The energy of a matched state never feels compressed. It feels unguarded. Even when intense, it carries an openness that your body recognizes as truth.

Now expand the awareness to the space around you. Let your field soften. You don't need to command anything. You're not trying to transmit a request. You're simply syncing to a frequency that already exists. Your role isn't to make it happen. It's to stop interfering.

This stillness—anchored in a felt sense of openness—is the ground where matching becomes possible. From here, movement, decision, and action will flow differently. You won't need to calculate your next step. It will rise out of you because the state itself is generative.

This is what most people miss when they're obsessed with scripting and visualizing. They're trying to *manipulate* reality into giving them something. Energy matching doesn't manipulate. It stabilizes. And when you're stable in the frequency of your next timeline, it cannot help but start shaping around you.

But this stability takes refinement. Your nervous system may try to pull you back. It may look for a problem to solve, a doubt to entertain, or a goal to chase. That's just the old identity checking if you're really ready to release it. You don't need to argue. Just return to the state.

Return to the breath. Return to the subtle openness. Let it become your new default, not just during practice, but while walking, emailing, speaking, eating. The more ordinary you let it become, the more power it holds.

Energy isn't something you send out into the universe like a flare. It's something you *become*. And that becoming is not loud. It's not effortful. It's precise, quiet, and internally clean.

If you find yourself needing to convince yourself of something, pause. Drop the words. Drop the visualization. Return to presence. Let the reality you're calling in become a tone that your body knows how to hold. That's alignment. And alignment is what reshapes timelines.

Let that be your ritual. Not forcing the vision, but training the frequency. Again and again, gently and honestly. Not for the result, but because you no longer need to pretend. You already feel it. You already are it. And that is when it starts appearing everywhere.

Script Rewrites That Don't Require Belief — Only Execution

One of the most dangerous myths in the personal development world is that you need to *believe* something in order to make it work. This belief-about-belief traps millions in an endless loop. They wait for internal conviction before they act, thinking that without certainty, the outcome will be flawed. But reality doesn't respond to belief the way people think. It responds to energetic commands embedded in behavior, attention, and state. Not the belief you proclaim, but the one your system enacts.

This is why the most powerful rewrites don't rely on belief. They bypass it. They embed new codes through execution. It's not about convincing the mind. It's about retraining the field.

If you wait to believe before you move, you'll stay in stasis. The version of you who already lives the new script doesn't believe differently. They *behave* differently. And those behaviors carry signals, and those signals produce feedback loops that rewire your identity and environment faster than belief ever could.

So how do you execute without belief? You start by detaching the emotional weight from the action. Most people hesitate not because they can't act, but because they've attached their entire identity to the outcome. They've made success or failure mean something about their worth, their destiny, their path. When you remove that interpretation, the action becomes light. It becomes clean. You're no longer trying to *prove* something. You're just rewriting.

And this is where command comes in.

You can speak to your field without waiting to feel ready. You can issue a directive that isn't emotional but structural. You don't need to believe that it's going to work. You only need to perform the action in a way that bypasses hesitation and marks a new trajectory. This is not about affirmations. It's not about repeating sentences in a mirror and hoping they eventually "sink in." It's about issuing a command that overrides the loop. Not once, but as a ritual of interruption.

Execution precedes evidence. And evidence reconditions the system.

There's a reason highly disciplined people often seem less conflicted internally. It's not because they started with belief. It's because their consistent action recalibrated their nervous system to accept new defaults. They acted long enough for the inner voice to catch up.

What you say to yourself doesn't matter if your actions disagree. The command ritual bypasses inner chatter entirely. It doesn't argue with doubt. It doesn't try to reframe fear. It simply moves.

This is not suppression. It's replacement. Doubt cannot survive in a body that acts as if it already knows. Not pretends. *Acts*. There is a difference.

Before we go into the ritual itself, pause here and reflect: where in your life are you still waiting to feel ready before you take action? Where are you trying to "believe harder" instead of moving cleaner? Where have you let the illusion of inner clarity delay what could have already shifted?

The rewrite starts the moment you stop needing belief as permission. And when you stop needing permission, the field starts listening. It has no choice. Execution is language. Movement is a command. That's the layer most people never access.

You don't need to convince yourself. You need to code yourself.

This is the point where the command ritual enters. Think of it not as a motivation technique, but as a system override. It is structured to bypass the intellectual gatekeeping of the conscious mind, and to speak directly to the subconscious through state-based repetition and embodied movement.

This ritual has three parts: command, confirmation, and convergence.

1. Command

You begin by naming the new script in its clearest form. It must be short, precise, and direct. Not a wish. A directive. For example:

"I operate with decisive clarity."

"My energy reshapes the room."

"Clients are drawn to my signal."

These are not affirmations for self-soothing. They are anchors for energetic precision. Say them *aloud*, with a steady, neutral tone. The voice should be calm, not dramatic. Authority does not yell. It simply transmits.

Repeat the command three times, once standing still, once while moving (walking or pacing), and once while holding eye contact with your reflection, not to believe it, but to *witness yourself issuing it*. The act of speaking it through motion breaks the habitual stasis of inner loops.

2. Confirmation

This is the step most people skip. You anchor the command by linking it to a micro-action that confirms it *in real time*. You do not wait for a sign from the outside. You generate it. If your command is about clarity, the action could be deleting old tasks and writing a single focus. If it's about influence, it might be reaching out to someone you've been avoiding. If it's about wealth, perhaps it's reviewing your account without fear.

The action doesn't prove the command is true. It *proves that the loop is no longer in charge*. This is what reshapes identity from the root: action that carries a different signal than your past version would have transmitted.

3. Convergence

Now, you collapse the gap. Most people keep their future self at a distance. The command ritual ends by merging with that version *now*. After the command and action, you sit still and breathe with your eyes closed. Ask: "What part of me already lives this script?"

Wait. Let the answer rise. It might be a memory, an image, or a physical feeling. Let that version of you take over. Not in theory. In sensation. In attitude. In subtle posture. That's the convergence point.

You are not programming your future. You are returning to alignment with the version that already holds the frequency you claimed.

This ritual is not meant to be done once. It's a daily cut into the loop. A precision blade. Done consistently, it rewires the field of expectation around you. You begin to respond to life with less friction and more inevitability. Opportunities don't just arise. You start stepping into them earlier, clearer, faster.

Belief becomes irrelevant because embodiment replaces it. You are no longer hoping for a shift. You are living from it.

This is the deeper script rewrite. Not tied to emotional hype. Not dependent on validation. Not limited by yesterday's narrative. Only executed, and therefore real.

Remember: belief is a result, not a requirement. When you act as the new code, the world adjusts. The game bends. Not because you forced it, but because you finally stopped waiting to believe. And now, it obeys.

Chapter 9. The Feedback Loop: How Reality Mirrors the Script in You

Your Life as a Live-Running Program

You are not living life. You are running a program called "life" that executes itself based on an underlying script you didn't consciously write.

Most people confuse the content of their life with its code. They see events, relationships, and routines as real, independent things, when in truth they are outputs—surface-level expressions of a deeper source code. That source code is your subconscious programming, shaped by repetition, emotion, language, and association. And like a running software, it doesn't pause just because you notice it. It continues, silently and precisely, executing line after line unless interrupted with intention.

The problem is not that your code is flawed. The problem is that it's outdated. Parts of it were installed when you were six. Other parts were absorbed unconsciously through family patterns, cultural messaging, or repeated failure. Each fragment of code holds a rule: "This is who I am," "This is what's possible," "This is how life responds to me." These rules form the internal operating system that your external life obeys.

You can try to override this through willpower, positive thinking, or intense motivation, but if the root code hasn't changed, the old program simply reruns itself as soon as your energy dips. That's why breakthroughs collapse. That's why new habits fade. The code never left.

Once you see your life as a live-running program, the goal changes. You no longer chase better outcomes by force. You study the code in real time and begin injecting edits while it's running.

This is not about obsessively analyzing yourself. It's about becoming aware of cause-and-effect loops while you are inside them.

For example, imagine a conversation where someone criticizes you. You feel a familiar contraction in your chest. Your mind quickly generates an internal command: "I need to defend myself or shut down." That moment is not random. It's code activating. You've run that script before. The contraction is not just emotional. It's part of a real-time execution sequence.

If unbroken, it leads to a predictable output—withdrawal, people-pleasing, aggression, or retreat.

This is where your power lies: in catching the script mid-execution and deciding to respond from outside the loop.

This requires neither perfect self-awareness nor endless analysis. What it does require is a kind of presence that feels mechanical at first, but becomes fluid with practice. You start to recognize signals as live code points. That sigh? A script trigger. That tight jaw? Script anchor. That sense of being stuck? A looping instruction.

To begin working with this, you must first become a watcher of your patterns without identifying with them. You are not the code. You are the programmer who can begin editing it.

The shift happens not when you fight the program, but when you begin to observe it from the outside without getting caught inside its momentum. That means noticing what the program is doing while it's doing it, instead of after it has already played out. And the only way to do that consistently is to bring structure to your awareness.

Let's introduce a reflection tool that acts as a kind of debugger. You use it not to judge your behavior, but to trace the invisible architecture behind it. This is not a journaling routine meant to process emotions. It's a practical system to extract code from action.

Reflection Tool: Code Tracing Sequence

This tool is most effective when used immediately after any moment where you feel off, reactive, stuck, or out of alignment. It can be used in writing or mentally, but writing often slows the mind down enough to reveal what's actually operating.

Ask yourself, one by one:

1. **What did I just do or feel?**

    This locks the moment in place before your mind rewrites it. Be specific. Don't just say "I felt bad." Say, "I avoided replying to the message and felt a wave of pressure in my chest."

2. **What internal command just ran?**

   There is always a hidden instruction behind your behavior. It might sound like: "Avoid conflict," "Don't be seen," "You're going to mess this up," "You have to fix this now." Let it surface. You don't need to fix it. Just see it.

3. **Where have I seen this loop before?**

   If the response is repetitive, there's a thread that connects this moment to a past one. Follow it. Maybe it happens every time you speak with authority figures. Maybe it's the same shutdown that occurs in creative work. Track it back. Pattern recognition is power.

4. **What part of me benefits from keeping this script running?**

   Even harmful scripts usually serve a protective function. Ask what fear or belief this program is trying to protect. Often, it's protecting you from rejection, exposure, failure, or shame. Name the benefit clearly so you can choose whether you still want it.

5. **What would a new instruction look like?**

   Do not try to write a perfect affirmation. Just consider: if this was a piece of code I could rewrite, what would I insert instead? For example, instead of "I must avoid being wrong," the new line might be "I allow clarity to emerge through discomfort." The goal is not to believe the new line instantly. The goal is to define it, so the old one is no longer running invisibly.

This process rewires your relationship to your own programming. You begin seeing that every reaction you label as "me" is actually a conditioned instruction that can be rewritten. This is not psychological excavation. It is system debugging. You are learning to see behavior as output, not identity. The deeper you go into this reflection process, the more clearly you begin to feel where your program lives in the body. You'll notice certain thoughts are tied to tension in your chest, certain phrases lock your jaw, certain decisions trigger a shutdown in your stomach. That's not random. That's compiled code running somatically. The nervous system carries the script, because it has been trained through repetition to execute it on command.

What this means is that the moment you slow down enough to witness the program with precision, it loses part of its power. Programs only stay dominant when they run invisibly. The act of observation itself creates a slight pause in the script, a flicker of choice where there used to be compulsion. In that space, even before anything changes, something rewires.

You will still fall back into loops. That's part of the process. But now, when you fall, you will see it. And every time you see it, you shorten its life. Every time you trace the pattern, you weaken its authority. Not through force. Through awareness applied consistently.

Eventually, the old code doesn't get deleted. It gets bypassed. Your system starts to execute a different set of instructions, even in the same environment. You are no longer reacting from memory. You are choosing from clarity.

And that's when you stop running the script, and the script starts responding to you.

Interpreting the Signs: When Reality Glitches Are Showing You the Code

There are moments when reality seems to misfire. A word is repeated back to you within seconds of thinking it. A song you haven't heard in years starts playing right after you remember someone from your past. You see numbers that feel like they're trying to tell you something. These are not accidents. They are not hallucinations. They are not "just coincidences." They are echoes—intentional reverberations within the structure of your personal reality script.

Reality glitches are not errors. They are overlays—brief lapses where the edges of the simulation become visible. Most people dismiss them. They're trained to explain them away, to maintain the illusion that the world is solid, rational, and fully mechanical. But to those who are ready, these moments offer something rare: a direct glimpse of the code behind the screen.

To interpret these signs, you need to understand the system they're running in. Reality isn't a flat sequence of external events. It is a multidimensional response to your internal frequency. Every image, every encounter, every disruption is filtered through your perceptual field. So when something "glitches," it's not just random—it's surfacing from the intersection between your subconscious and the architecture of the field you're in.

There's a reason the same symbols appear over and over when someone is going through a shift. Numbers like 111, 333, or 911. Repeating names. Sudden emotional flashes tied to songs or phrases. It's because the subconscious communicates in symbols, not logic. And when it detects an inconsistency between the self you're running and the self you're ready to step into, it begins to break through the program.

The moment you notice a glitch, you are already outside the script—if only for a second. That's the window. The question is: will you dismiss it or decode it?

Decoding doesn't mean overanalyzing or forcing a meaning onto everything you see. It means listening. Being available. Staying open without trying to control the message. The field isn't testing you. It's prompting you. It's offering real-time feedback that your conscious mind can't yet produce on its own.

Let's get practical.

Symbol Interpretation Practice: The 3-Level Decode

Whenever you notice a sign, pattern, or glitch that strikes you as meaningful—even subtly—run it through the following filter.

1. Surface Symbol

What is the literal content? This is what actually happened. The number you saw, the phrase you heard, the visual repetition. Note it clearly, without interpreting. You are anchoring the raw data before the mind starts bending it.

2. Emotional Echo

What did you feel in that moment, before the mind tried to explain it? Did something tighten? Open? Was there a flicker of excitement, dread, or déjà vu? This is the subconscious resonance. Don't brush past it. Your body often understands the symbol before your logic does.

3. Internal Inquiry

Ask: "What part of me is this symbol reflecting right now?" Do not try to be mystical. Be honest. For example, if you keep seeing the same name, ask: "What part of my past or identity is still unresolved here?" If the same number appears, ask what it meant to you the first time it became significant. If an old song plays, ask what story you once attached to it.

You are not asking for external answers. You are using the symbol as a diagnostic tool for your internal state. You're not interpreting the universe. You're interpreting your alignment.

This decoding practice isn't about collecting signs like trophies. It's about developing fluency in the language of the field. And once you understand that the field speaks in symbols—tailored to your personal archive—you stop asking, "Is this real?" and start asking, "What is this pointing to in me?" When you become fluent in this internal decoding process, symbols stop being curiosities and start becoming instructions. You realize that the field is not random. It is reactive. And the signs it shows you are not predictions, but projections of your own energetic posture. They're not telling you the future. They're telling you what script you're currently running.

For example, a person constantly encountering the symbol of death—be it in media, dreams, or synchronicities—is not being warned of physical death. More often, it signals the collapse of an identity or belief structure. Something that no longer serves is being disassembled. But if that person fears the symbol and resists it, the collapse becomes chaotic. If they read it correctly, it becomes a portal to transformation.

The way you relate to these signs determines their effect. If you try to assign them universal meaning, you miss the point. A crow may symbolize death for one person and freedom for another. The significance lies in what your subconscious has already associated with that symbol. You are not interpreting the field. You are interpreting your own coded reality within it. This is why journaling symbolic patterns can be a powerful form of self-debugging. You begin to see loops in your inner world you would never catch with pure thought. You start to notice that certain patterns arise when you're nearing a decision, resisting a shift, or denying something you already know deep down. These patterns are like breadcrumbs scattered by a deeper part of you, hoping you'll trace them back to the part of the script that needs rewriting.

What most people call "the universe speaking" is not some distant, external force intervening in your life. It is your own awareness, filtered through a symbolic mirror. It is your higher intelligence using the language of imagery and pattern to slip past the guards of the rational mind. If you only listen with logic, you miss the message. But if you feel your way through it, the meaning lands directly, like a download.

This is also where you must be careful not to fall into obsession. Not every repetition is a message. Not every symbol demands decoding. If you try to find meaning in everything, you dilute your sensitivity. The key is resonance. If a symbol moves something in you—if it stops you, wakes you, shakes you—then it's for you. If it leaves you cold, let it pass.

To sharpen this skill, begin to treat the world as a living interface. Everything in your field is a potential message. Not because it's all important, but because your perception decides what is activated. And once a symbol activates something in you, that activation reveals where your energy is tethered. The glitch is never the message. The shift in you is.

You're not looking for signs to tell you what to do. You're learning to recognize how you're being shaped by what you're already noticing. The signs don't show up to give you power. They show up once you've begun to claim it. They don't change your path. They confirm that you've reached a threshold.

Here is a final layer: signs often appear *before* the conscious mind realizes a choice has been made. You may still think you're undecided, but the field begins responding to a deeper internal signal. This is why signs seem to lead the way. It's not because they are ahead of you. It's because the field is tracking your most honest frequency, not your surface-level indecision.

So if you're seeing symbols, if reality is glitching, if patterns are repeating so clearly they're almost loud, take it seriously—but not rigidly. Don't fall into superstition. Don't outsource your intuition to omens. Instead, treat them like breadcrumbs from your own code, placed there by a part of you that is already beyond the loop. Each time you follow one with presence, it leads you not to an answer, but to a clearer version of yourself. That is the real message. That is the only sign that ever mattered.

Debugging: Rewriting Scripts That Keep Attracting the Wrong Loops

You can feel it when it happens. A moment that seems new begins unfolding, yet it carries a strange familiarity. The faces may change. The setting is different. But the emotional weather is the same. The same feeling of not being chosen. The same tension before things fall apart. The same cycle of trying, striving, collapsing. And a quiet voice inside you says, *Not again.*

This is the mark of a loop. Not a singular event, but a self-reinforcing code structure that plays out as a lived experience. And no matter how much action you take, how many boundaries you set, how hard you try to stay positive, you keep getting pulled back into it. That's because loops are not changed by force. They are rewritten by debugging the script that sustains them.

What keeps most people trapped is the belief that the loop exists "out there." They believe if they just find the right partner, job, community, or opportunity, the loop will break. But the external is only responding to the internal script. Until the code that *attracts* the loop is identified and altered, the pattern will persist. Not because the universe is cruel, but because it is consistent. It cannot reflect what has not been reprogrammed.

Loops often form around unprocessed emotional anchors. These anchors become internal commands, written in the language of survival. For example, a child who learns that love must be earned through performance may unconsciously write a script that says, *Only when I prove my worth will I receive care.* That child becomes an adult who attracts relationships that demand endless effort and offer conditional affection. It is not a conscious choice. It is a programmed expectation.

To break the loop, you must move from symptom management to script exposure. That means identifying the core command that is running underneath the surface. And this requires more than journaling or affirmations. It requires slowing down enough to notice the moment the loop begins—while it's happening—and intercepting it at the level of belief. A powerful starting point is recognizing your loop's emotional fingerprint. Every loop has one. It's a sensation that appears early in the sequence. It may feel like tightness in the chest, a drop in the stomach, a buzzing behind the eyes. These somatic signals are not random. They are access points to the code.

Let's say the moment someone doesn't text back, a familiar hollowness sets in. It's not just disappointment. It's the reactivation of the belief *I am not wanted unless I perform or pursue.* That's the loop initializing. If you don't catch it, you'll start running the usual responses: self-doubt, overexplaining, chasing, emotional collapse. But if you catch it—if you feel the sensation and pause—you can trace the loop back to its root and begin rewriting.

This is where most teachings fall short. They offer surface-level tools without addressing the underlying command line. You cannot override a script you haven't read. You must first *see* it with precision. Not to judge it. Not to shame it. But to understand why it was written in the first place. Every loop had a purpose once. It protected you. It kept you safe in environments that were not safe. But what protected you then may be limiting you now.

In the next section, we will walk through the Loop Exit Protocol—a practical, repeatable method to intercept, expose, and rewrite the script while the loop is live. You'll learn how to identify the moment of activation, surface the internal command, and insert a new directive into your system while the old one is running.

Let's move into the step-by-step.

Loop Exit Protocol

1. Name the Emotional Activation

The first signal is not mental. It's physical. Before the loop gains momentum, the body signals its arrival. Tension in the neck, tightness in the chest, heat behind the eyes, a sudden drop in your gut. These are not incidental. They are the system alerting you to an old command reactivating. When this happens, name it out loud or internally with specificity. Not just "I feel bad." But "This feels like that moment when I was left out." Or "This is the ache of being unseen again." The more precisely you name it, the more clearly you access the entry point of the loop.

2. Pause the Default Reaction

Every loop has a chain reaction. Naming is not enough. The power comes in pausing. This pause does not mean suppressing or avoiding. It means interrupting the habitual trajectory long enough to introduce conscious intervention.

In that pause, do not ask what you want to do. Ask what the loop expects you to do. What behavior, if you followed it, would strengthen the pattern? Is it overexplaining? Withdrawing? Controlling? Overgiving? Once identified, resist enacting that behavior for at least 90 seconds. This moment is the rewrite window.

3. Trace the Command

Now ask, "What belief would someone have to hold to act like this?" Let the answer emerge without editing. It might be something like "I have to fix things to be safe" or "No one stays unless I keep proving my value." These are not flaws in your character. They are fragments of survival code. They once helped you adapt. But adaptation is not alignment. And it's time to upgrade the code.

4. Speak a Disruptive Directive

Do not replace the old command with a surface affirmation. Instead, speak a directive that disrupts the loop at its energetic core. It must be short, sharp, and carry a frequency that doesn't ask for permission. It should sound like a line of code, not a wish.

Examples:
- "This is not my timeline anymore."
- "I no longer chase echoes."
- "That belief ends with me."

Say it with finality. Say it with breath in your chest. Not to convince yourself. But to signal a new instruction to the field.

5. Perform a Micro-Shift

After the directive is spoken, you must embody a signal of shift. Not a grand gesture. A micro-action that contradicts the loop's expectation. If the loop expects you to apologize again, remain silent and grounded. If the loop expects you to collapse, stand upright and breathe deeper. If it expects you to pursue, walk away without flinching.

This movement locks the rewrite into the nervous system. Without it, the directive stays conceptual. But once the body participates, the loop recognizes that the code has changed.

6. Observe Without Needing Immediate Proof

Your job is not to force the universe to reflect the change instantly. Your job is to *maintain the new instruction* regardless of whether the external validates it yet. This is where many collapse. They say the directive, take the micro-shift, and then immediately look for signs that "it worked." That looking is part of the old loop—chasing certainty to feel safe. Let go of the need for proof and instead track your alignment.

You'll notice that something begins to shift. Sometimes subtly. Sometimes drastically. People behave differently. Events reroute. The loop starts to dissolve—not because you forced reality to obey, but because you stopped coding the same structure into the system.

Loops only survive where old energy continues to feed them. The Loop Exit Protocol isn't just about change. It's about reclaiming authorship over the invisible code you've been running without knowing it. The more precisely and repeatedly you run this protocol, the more permanent the rewrites become.

And when they do, something strange happens. You'll try to enter the old loop again, and it won't load. The doorway will be gone. The bait won't catch. The code will be clean.

Part IV. Walking as the Programmer

There is a point in this work where something subtle, but irreversible, begins to happen.
You stop chasing insight and start moving from a different center. You stop trying to fix the program and begin writing it. You stop asking what is true and start deciding what becomes true through you.
This part of the process is not about intensity. It's not about stacking more rituals or learning another method. It's about stabilization. It's about walking as if the shift already happened, because in many ways, it has. You've altered the source code. Now, this part is about anchoring it.
To walk as the programmer means the script no longer runs you. It responds to you. It reflects what you permit, project, and transmit through your presence. You've stepped beyond the debugging phase. You're now testing live code in real-time environments. Not with the fragility of "hoping it sticks," but with the calm certainty that the field is already responding. Because it is.
But this is where many relapse.
When old loops no longer appear, a strange emptiness can take their place. You may notice a silence where noise used to be. A stillness where chaos once gave you a role to play. You may even question who you are without the old friction. And this is where the deeper initiation begins.
Walking as the programmer is not a performance. It's not about pretending to be powerful. It's about not shrinking when your frequency has already shifted. It's about holding your new signal in the face of people, places, and timelines that still echo the old you—and choosing not to answer the call.
The chapters that follow are not just tools. They are integrations. They are about reclaiming authorship without needing validation. Rewiring reality not from desperation, but from design. Speaking code not to impress, but to align. Acting not for proof, but as a declaration of who you've become.
You are not fixing. You are architecting.
You are not waiting. You are already writing.
You are not becoming the version. You are embodying the code.

Let's walk.

Chapter 10. Conscious Frequency Control

Why You Can't "Stay High Vibe" and Why You Don't Have To

If you've been in the manifestation space for long enough, you've likely heard it: "Stay high vibe." "Protect your energy." "Keep your frequency elevated at all costs." The advice sounds empowering. But for many, it becomes a silent burden. A source of guilt when they feel off. A reason to repress emotion. A subtle form of self-surveillance that reinforces shame instead of liberation.

The truth is not only that you can't stay "high vibe" all the time — you're not supposed to.

Human emotional range is not a glitch in your system. It's part of your design. Every feeling, every state, every shift in mood carries data. And more importantly, carries access. The most powerful upgrades don't come from hovering in an artificial state of bliss. They come from moving through the internal noise without resistance, without story, and without self-rejection.

Trying to "stay high vibe" at all costs often does the opposite of what you intend. It forces you to compartmentalize parts of yourself that are inconvenient to your image of what it means to be spiritual, aligned, or evolved. But alignment doesn't mean hovering above life. It means allowing energy to move cleanly through you without identification. It means meeting what arises — fully — without collapsing into it or pushing it away. That's where real frequency shift happens. Not in avoiding the low, but in not attaching a false meaning to it. Not in rejecting discomfort, but in refusing to narrate it as failure.

Energy naturally fluctuates. Like breath. Like seasons. Like tides. You're not here to hold a static vibration. You're here to be the stable presence through which waves pass and transform. Presence is the constant. Not the mood. Not the feeling. Not the spike of euphoria or the dip of fatigue. When you understand this, you stop fighting your own rhythms. You stop performing alignment. And you start living from it.

There's a deeper danger in the "stay high vibe" dogma: it subtly equates feeling good with being on the right path, and feeling bad with being off it. But some of your biggest initiations will come cloaked in friction, disorientation, or loss. Some of the most aligned decisions will temporarily destabilize your comfort. If your only compass is how good something feels in the moment, you'll abandon the process before the upgrade completes.

This is especially true when rewriting subconscious scripts. Old timelines don't dissolve quietly. They resist. They echo. Sometimes they scream. And if you interpret that as "I must be out of alignment," you'll fall back into the very loop you were breaking.

Your job isn't to chase an ideal frequency. It's to become aware of the one you're broadcasting, without judgment, and choose your signal from there. This is not about suppressing fear or pretending sadness is gone. It's about knowing how to hold space for them without letting them code your reality. You're not broken when you feel low. You're not failing when you feel blocked. You're not misaligned when your system is recalibrating. You are simply in a layer of the code that is asking to be seen, acknowledged, and integrated without story.

You don't need to escape a low state. You need to become aware of its language before it becomes a script. This is what changes everything. Instead of treating discomfort as something to override, you start relating to it as information. You stop layering interpretation on top of sensation. You stop turning a temporary wave into a lifelong identity.

The fear you feel isn't dangerous. The sadness isn't permanent. The anger isn't evidence of failure. They are all frequencies trying to communicate, not dominate. The problem starts when you fuse them with meaning. "I feel scared" quietly turns into "I am not safe here." "I feel blocked" becomes "I must not be meant for this." These internal translations write your energetic code more than the emotion itself ever could.

That's why chasing "high vibe" can become a trap. Not because high states are wrong, but because when you idolize them, you build resistance to everything else. That resistance creates friction in your field, tension in your body, and distortion in your manifestation signals. You don't attract based on what you pretend to feel. You attract based on what your system believes to be safe. If you only allow yourself to feel good when conditions are perfect, you train your nervous system to avoid growth. You teach it that expansion is conditional.

Real energetic mastery isn't about holding a smile through chaos. It's about letting the chaos move through you without rearranging your identity. It's about keeping your frequency anchored even as your emotional weather shifts. And that starts with decoupling emotional states from meaning. You feel heavy? Fine. But don't tell yourself it means you're broken. You feel low? That's not a curse. It's a signal. You get to respond, not collapse.

This is where self-honesty becomes a tool of liberation. Not to punish yourself, but to free yourself from unconscious patterning. What if you allowed every emotion to be what it is, without narrative? What if you stopped trying to reach the "correct" state and instead attuned to what was real? You would find that clarity emerges. Not as a performance. As a natural result of inner coherence.

You're not here to force frequency. You're here to remember your role as the signal carrier. When your system learns that all states are survivable, all emotions are permitted, and none of them can hijack your core, you stop fearing your own humanness. You stop needing to control every moment of your internal world. This is the energetic foundation of power: neutrality, not numbness. Presence, not performance.

From here, your nervous system can finally rest. Your field can finally stabilize. And ironically, your overall frequency rises not because you forced it, but because you stopped resisting what was already trying to move through.

You didn't come here to hover above your life. You came to encode your life from the inside out. Not by rejecting contrast, but by integrating it. Not by chasing only the light, but by learning how to hold both shadow and clarity without losing access to who you are.

You are not meant to be high vibe.

You are meant to be clear.

And clarity always outcodes emotion. Always.

Tuning Instead of Forcing: Setting the Internal Dial

There's a critical difference between trying to feel different and learning how to tune yourself into alignment. Most people never pause to notice the distinction. They spend years pushing themselves into better moods, higher thoughts, more productive mindsets. It's all effortful. It's all upstream. The entire approach is built on resistance — which paradoxically hardens the very state they're trying to change.

Tuning, on the other hand, is subtle. It doesn't rely on force. It doesn't require pretending. It isn't about bypassing what you're currently experiencing. Instead, it's about shifting the signal you're sending out by engaging with your inner system in a new way.

Think of your internal state as a frequency band. You're always broadcasting something — not necessarily in your words or your posture, but in the underlying code you emit. This code is energetic, somatic, and perceptual. It lives in how you hold yourself, how you interpret sensation, how you expect things to unfold. That's the signal the external world responds to. That's the field that pulls in resonance.

When your inner dial is set to scarcity, every opportunity looks like a risk. Every pause feels like failure. Every silence is misread as rejection. Not because it is — but because that's what your frequency is tuned to interpret. This is why changing your life requires more than action. It requires subtle recalibration. Tuning is not about producing an entirely different broadcast all at once. It's about turning the internal dial one click at a time until the signal shifts.

To begin this process, you don't start with willpower. You start with presence. What are you broadcasting right now? Not what are you thinking, not what are you hoping — but what are you radiating? What are you bracing for? What outcome are you silently expecting, even while telling yourself you want something else?

This is where most people lose the game: they act from desire while remaining tuned to fear. They speak of expansion while their bodies hum with contraction. They visualize success while their nervous systems cling to survival. And because the field responds to the deepest signal — not the loudest — results often match the unspoken broadcast, not the spoken intention.

Tuning starts with sensation. Not because you have to feel a certain way, but because your body holds the current frequency. Instead of fixing the feeling, you get curious about it. You name the texture. You slow the rhythm. You stop rushing to improve anything. The moment you do this, you interrupt the compulsion to override. And that's when something new becomes possible: space.

In this space, you're no longer reacting. You're no longer performing. You're listening. And that's when you can start to adjust the dial. Not by pushing toward a better state, but by inviting in something slightly closer to coherence. Just one shift. Just one breath. Just one layer of ease beneath the noise. This is where real influence over your internal state begins.

What most people miss is that tuning isn't about creating a specific emotion. It's about stabilizing a frequency that aligns with the version of you who is already beyond the loop. This frequency doesn't always feel "good" in the traditional sense. It feels stable. Clear. Unrushed. Unattached. That's the power source behind true presence.

The shift begins when you stop resisting the signal you're currently broadcasting. Resistance binds the frequency. Curiosity loosens it. Once you drop the judgment of your internal state, even if it's dense or foggy, you gain access to something far more important than feeling better: awareness. From here, tuning becomes a matter of choosing clarity over control.

The internal dial is not a metaphor. It's a felt interface. You access it through the body, through breath, through the way you relate to what is happening right now. You don't need a perfect mood or polished mindset to use it. You just need to sense where your current signal is anchored and create the smallest opening for movement.

Here's how to engage the tuning process:

Step One: Sensory Scan

Sit or stand without trying to adjust your posture. Let yourself be as you are. Close your eyes if it helps eliminate visual noise. Then begin a slow scan from your feet upward. Notice where there's tension, buzzing, pressure, numbness, or speed. Not to fix it. Just to meet it. Give each region a few seconds of direct attention. No commentary. Just sensation.

Step Two: Frequency Labeling

Ask yourself, *If this state had a frequency, what would it be saying?* This might sound like a thought, but you're looking for tone. For example, it might say: *Something bad is about to happen.* Or *I'm about to get rejected.* Or *I can't keep up.* Again, the point is not to believe the content. You're just identifying the underlying broadcast. You can't shift what you won't name.

Step Three: Micro-Adjustment

Now, with your full presence on that frequency, find one area in your body that is holding the strongest part of that tone. It may be your chest, gut, jaw, or even hands. Once you've located it, breathe into it gently and ask a question that opens the dial: *What is one degree of ease I can invite here?* Not relief. Not escape. Just one degree of ease. Wait. Don't rush. Let your body answer.

The shift will often be subtle: a loosening in your breath, a drop in mental static, a slight change in internal texture. These micro-adjustments are more powerful than emotional spikes because they're sustainable. They mark a new point on the dial. Once you feel that one-degree shift, you're no longer locked in the old broadcast.

Step Four: Anchor the New Setting

To solidify the new signal, speak something out loud that reflects the frequency you just accessed. Not a mantra. Not an affirmation. A clean sentence that emerges from the shift. Something like *I am not rushing* or *I can meet this from stillness.* Keep it simple and direct. The act of vocalizing it lets the field register the new setting as your current code.

Tuning is an ongoing process, not a one-time event. You're not aiming for a perfect state. You're learning to become fluent in your own broadcast. This fluency gives you leverage. It lets you enter any situation — conversation, decision, challenge — from the setting that serves your next level, not your default loop.

You'll know you've tuned effectively when your internal environment becomes less urgent. You'll feel less like you have to fix something and more like you're inside a clear field where responses emerge naturally. This clarity doesn't just improve outcomes. It collapses unnecessary resistance, opens creative pathways, and recalibrates what people unconsciously mirror back to you.

You don't need to wait until you feel powerful to send a powerful signal. You just need to stop transmitting from survival when you're no longer in danger. The internal dial is always available. You don't have to force it. You just have to return to it, feel the current setting, and shift by one honest degree. That's enough. That's the gateway to a new script.

Guarding Your Field: Eliminating Energetic Backdoors

Most people walk around wide open. Not in a beautiful, radiant way — in a leaky, unconsciously exposed way. Their field is filled with impressions that aren't theirs. Thoughts they didn't choose. Agreements they never consciously made. This happens because most people never learned how to *guard* their field — not with force or fear, but with clarity.

Your energetic field is not a metaphor. It's a real, living intelligence that surrounds and permeates your body. It absorbs, mirrors, transmits, and interacts with other fields constantly. Every time you enter a space, connect with a person, scroll past an image, or speak a word, your field shifts. The problem isn't that your field is responsive. The problem is that most people are *unaware* of what they've allowed in.

Energetic backdoors are the subtle, often invisible openings that allow old scripts, external influences, and manipulative energies to enter and affect your system. They aren't always obvious. They can hide behind compliments. Behind "being nice." Behind the need to be understood, seen, or included. A backdoor is any opening through which your field gets programmed *without your permission.*

You might feel the effects of backdoors in the form of chronic fatigue after certain interactions, looping thoughts that didn't originate with you, strange guilt after saying no, or dreams that leave a residue of confusion. These are not random. They're traces of influence, signs that something entered your field through a door you forgot to close — or never knew was open.

The first step in eliminating backdoors is awareness of how and when your field is being entered. Most people assume energetic intrusion only happens in hostile environments. But the more dangerous ones happen in spaces where your guard is down — with people you love, teachers you trust, or content you consume when your mind is soft.

Start noticing when your body gives you a signal that something has touched your space. It might be a tightening in your solar plexus. A sudden drop in energy. A fog that appears after a conversation. These are not emotional reactions. They are field alerts. Learn to trust them.

The second step is to recognize the shape of the backdoor. Some common forms include:

- Seeking validation from someone who does not have the capacity to see you
- Overexplaining yourself in conversations where your truth is already known internally
- Entering agreements (spoken or unspoken) where your presence is used but your power is not honored
- Repeating phrases or ideas that don't originate from your own direct knowing, especially in spiritual or mindset spaces

These are not failures. They are invitations to close the openings and rewrite the permissions.

To seal a backdoor, you don't need to confront anyone. The shift happens in your field, not theirs. This is not about becoming hard or guarded. It's about becoming sovereign. Closing a backdoor means declaring that your field is no longer a passive receiver of other people's unresolved projections, desires, or distortions.

Before we move into the daily routine that helps guard your field, pause here. Let the concept settle. Begin noticing what you've tolerated without naming. What you've absorbed without questioning. What you've called "just how I am" that might actually be *someone else's residue* living in your space.

The most powerful fields are not the loudest. They are the cleanest. And cleanliness requires the courage to say no to anything that doesn't serve your clarity — not from fear, but from frequency. The kind of frequency that leaves no door unguarded.

Protecting your field is not about building walls. It's about setting the frequency so precisely that anything not aligned with your current signal simply cannot enter. That frequency doesn't come from hypervigilance. It comes from clarity. You're not pushing anything out. You're broadcasting something so pure and coherent that interference dissolves.

The key is not in shielding yourself all day long. That's reactive. What you want instead is a proactive routine that tunes your field to its natural baseline and clears foreign signatures before they embed. Think of it as energetic hygiene — subtle, precise, and powerful.

Daily Field Protection Routine: "Return and Reset"

1. **Enter Stillness**

   Set aside two to five minutes, preferably at the start or end of your day. Sit or stand in silence. No mantras. No visualizations. Just feel. Let your awareness drop beneath thought. Let your breath slow. The silence is not the absence of sound — it's the absence of distortion. This is the neutral space where you can hear what's actually yours.

2. **Scan the Field**

   With your awareness, begin scanning your body and energetic perimeter. Not with your mind, but with your inner sense. What feels like yours? What doesn't? You might notice images, phrases, or faces flash in your awareness. You don't need to analyze them. Just observe. Your system already knows what doesn't belong. Let it show you.

3. **Command the Return**

   Once you've identified foreign signatures, use your internal voice to speak a clear command. Something like: *"I return all energy, projections, and imprints that are not mine to their original source, neutralized and cleared. I retrieve all of my own energy now."* Say it from your core, not your throat. Feel the shift. Your words are not affirmations — they are actions.

4. **Seal the Field**

   After the return, imagine a subtle shift in your field's edges. You're not building a barrier. You're restoring integrity. The frequency becomes crystalline. Anything that doesn't match this signal can no longer interface. The field becomes quiet again, like water returning to stillness after a ripple.

5. **Reclaim Sovereignty**

   End the practice with a felt declaration: *"Only what serves my clarity, growth, and truth is allowed in. I walk as the sole programmer of my field."*
   Let this be your internal setting — not as a defense, but as a command.

You don't have to perform this routine rigidly every day, but the more you do, the more your field remembers what clean feels like. And once it remembers, anything foreign becomes instantly noticeable.

Some people will unconsciously test the new integrity of your field. That's not an attack. It's an echo of the old script asking, "Are you sure?" You don't need to convince anyone. Just hold the line. You'll notice certain conversations shift. Certain invitations lose their pull. You'll stop explaining yourself where before you felt obligated to. This is field-level debugging. And it happens silently.

You're not here to walk through life avoiding noise. You're here to walk through it untouched by noise that isn't yours. That requires presence. Not perfection. Presence is what lets you catch the moment a hook is offered — and decline it before it lands. Not with fear. With neutrality.

This isn't about becoming invisible or unavailable. It's about becoming precise. Your presence becomes unmistakable. Your frequency becomes sovereign. And the field around you stops being a sponge and starts being a signal.

That's when the game changes. Not because you fought for space. But because you *claimed it*.

Chapter 11. Script Collapse and Code Injection

The Moment of Rewrite: How to Collapse an Identity Mid-Loop

There's a split second in every reactive loop where time opens. A sliver between stimulus and response. Between the surge of an old identity trying to reassert itself and the choice to remain sovereign. That sliver is where the rewrite becomes possible. Not in the journal. Not in the vision board. Right there — mid-loop.

Most people miss it because they're inside the identity as it takes over. The self is overtaken by the script, and by the time awareness returns, the loop has already played out. Words have already left the mouth. The email has already been sent. The silence has already become avoidance. In those moments, it feels like the self is observing from a distance, unable to interrupt what's already set in motion. But that's not entirely true.

The loop only feels unstoppable because it recruits your full sense of identity. When the pattern arises, it doesn't come wearing a mask. It wears *you*. It speaks with your voice. It uses your memories, your logic, your urgency. That's what makes it so persuasive. It doesn't feel like a pattern — it feels like the only truth in the room. The compulsion is mistaken for clarity.

And yet, even inside that intensity, there is a flicker. The sensation that this moment has happened before. The breath that shortens. The jaw that tightens. The need to explain, defend, or disappear. The exact way your body prepares itself to reenact a script that no longer belongs to you. That's your entry point.

You can't collapse an identity you're still convinced is "you." Which means the work doesn't begin by fighting the loop. It begins by locating *which identity* is trying to drive the moment. Is it the one that believes it's always misunderstood? The one that compensates through control? The one that chases validation to avoid silence? Each one runs a different version of urgency. Each one speaks in a different tone.

But here's the key: the pattern only survives if it goes unrecognized. The moment you name it, you are no longer it. You are witnessing it. That shift in awareness is the first step of the collapse.

Disrupting the Loop in Real Time

This technique isn't complicated. It's not elegant. But it works. You don't need a sacred space or the right playlist. You just need a breath, a phrase, and a pause. You interrupt the signal before it completes the circuit.
Let's break down the components.

1. **The Breath**: Not a deep breath to calm yourself. A precise inhale that brings *presence* to the body. Short. Sharp. Intentional. Like snapping your awareness back into the now. It's not for relaxation. It's for disruption.

2. **The Phrase**: This is not an affirmation. It's a command. Something like, *"Not this version."* Or *"This is a loop, not me."* You say it inside, with authority. It's not about positive thinking. It's about code recognition. The phrase acts like a pattern breaker in the system. It creates a rupture in the expected trajectory.

3. **The Pause**: After the phrase, you stop moving for three to five seconds. No speaking. No typing. No acting. Just stillness. The loop is expecting your participation. When it doesn't get it, it begins to dissolve. The script needs your agreement. Remove the agreement, and the structure collapses.

This moment — the breath, the phrase, the pause — is the fulcrum point. You are neither fully inside the old identity nor fully outside it. You're in the void between. And that is exactly where the rewrite must occur.

The discomfort of this space is precisely why most people rush to fill it. The identity wants resolution. It wants to return to something familiar, even if it's destructive. It wants to complete the loop. But if you stay in the pause just a few seconds longer than you normally would, something starts to shift. The body begins to register the pattern without being consumed by it. The nervous system, momentarily unhooked from its preloaded response, enters a brief window of neuroplasticity. You are still feeling the heat, the charge, the tension — but you are no longer fusing with the role that usually acts it out.

This is the exact moment where a new command can be inserted.

It won't feel like a big transformation. It won't feel powerful or certain. It may feel awkward or even ridiculous at first. That's because the command is being dropped into unfamiliar territory. The system doesn't yet trust this version of you. It has no reference point for this level of interruption. Which is exactly why the command must be simple and unshakeable.

Something like:

"I don't need to respond from this identity."

"This script is expired."

"I collapse this loop now."

You're not speaking to another person. You're speaking directly to your own field. It's not a performance. It's an override. The moment you do this, you are no longer passively participating in the program. You are editing it. Most people try to change behavior after the fact. They reflect on what they wish they had said or done differently. But in the rewrite moment, you're no longer theorizing. You are standing at the junction where new choices can reroute an entire chain of cause and effect. It may not feel significant in the moment. But this single divergence shifts the code base for every future instance of that loop.

What happens next matters less than how you hold your internal signal. You may still feel emotion. You may still feel the old urge. But if you don't merge with the identity again — if you stay centered in the one who *chose* to intervene — the rewrite holds.

You are not trying to feel good. You are not trying to think differently. You are choosing not to embody a worn-out sequence. The feeling may still echo. The thoughts may still fire. But the actor has exited the stage. And without the actor, the scene loses its power.

Eventually, the pattern begins to dissolve not through suppression, but through disuse. The mind stops reaching for it. The body stops rehearsing it. Your system stops assigning it as a solution. And what replaces it is not always a clear identity — often it's simply space. A kind of neutrality where you don't need to be anyone at all.

This is power most people never access. Not because it's hidden, but because it requires discomfort. It requires letting go of the part of you that gets certainty from repetition. The loop may feel like protection, like safety, like righteousness. But it's only a shortcut that turns sovereignty into habit. To collapse a loop mid-script is to reclaim authorship in the messiest moment. Not after the calm returns. Not when you've had time to process. Right there, inside the heat. Inside the urgency. Inside the noise.

And when you prove to yourself that you can do this once, something profound changes. The loop begins to anticipate disruption. It weakens. It loses authority. And in its place, you begin to build something far more potent — a self that is no longer reacting to scripts, but writing new ones with precision, presence, and choice.

Injecting New Commands: Replacing Repetition with Power

Most people live in a script that was never consciously chosen. Thoughts repeat. Emotional reactions run in cycles. Behaviors seem spontaneous, but they follow deep, embedded sequences. These aren't just habits. They're running commands — inherited, absorbed, and reinforced over time. If left untouched, they replicate themselves endlessly, even when you try to "change your life." The reason is simple: repetition is the default. Without a new directive, the mind reverts to what it knows.

But what if you could speak directly to the system? Not through long journaling, not through abstract affirmations, but through precision-coded command lines that your subconscious recognizes immediately?

This is not about shouting affirmations at a mirror. It's not about emotional hype. It's about injecting new code into a live-running environment.

That environment is your perception. The lens through which you interpret every moment. And that lens, as malleable as it is, runs on embedded instructions. You can think of these like "if-this-then-that" statements:

- If I'm criticized, then I shut down.
- If I'm not validated, then I withdraw.
- If I don't feel in control, then I panic.

These are not conscious decisions. They are embedded scripts. And the key to altering them isn't to analyze them endlessly, but to *overwrite* them.

That's what a code injection is.

A code injection is a short, precise, energetically charged directive that replaces an existing sequence. It bypasses the intellectual filters and speaks directly to the part of you that's been repeating the old pattern. The goal is not to convince yourself. The goal is to *input* a new instruction so clearly that the body and perception field begin to obey.

Here's the paradox: it doesn't need to feel true in order to work. It needs to be *held* with intention.

If you wait until you feel powerful to inject a powerful command, you'll be trapped in the same loop. The most effective moment for injection is when the system is destabilized — when the old command is exposed and trembling. That's when the rewrite has the most access.

The process starts by identifying the loop trigger. What's the sequence that keeps hijacking your state? You don't need to know its full history. You only need to see the moment it starts.

Maybe it's a glance from someone you perceive as superior. Maybe it's the silence that follows when you express an idea. Maybe it's the slight shift in tone from someone you want approval from. Whatever the entry point, your job is to catch it right there — not ten minutes later, not after the spiral, but in the split second before the body takes over.

This is where the code injection tool enters.

It's not a script you read. It's not a mantra. It's a designed input — a phrase or command that collapses the default and replaces it with intentional architecture. It must be sharp, frictionless, and emotionally clean. That means it doesn't argue with the old loop. It doesn't try to "fix" or "correct" anything. It simply *replaces*.

At this point, you're not trying to be logical or inspirational. You're switching systems. What you input here becomes the architecture of your next moment.

The Code Injection Tool: How to Construct It

To inject a new command, you need a clean, intentional phrase that operates like a directive to your system. Think of it not as a motivational statement but as a line of source code. It's not there to convince you of something. It's there to execute.

There are three criteria for a powerful injection:

1. **It bypasses your story.**

    The injection must not debate your history, identity, or trauma. It's not interested in what happened. It operates in the now. Instead of, "I am healing from rejection," try "I choose presence over approval." The first statement is autobiographical. The second is functional. You're programming behavior, not narrating emotion.

2. **It doesn't require belief.**

    You don't need to believe it fully. It doesn't need to feel "true." Its job is not emotional resonance but energetic dominance. When you hold the command as a focal point — even if the body resists — you're redirecting the current. "I operate from clarity now" is not a request. It's a switch. It's a line of instruction that begins to pull the nervous system in a new direction.

3. **It's simple and live-actionable.**

    The command must be usable in real time. That means it needs to be short, sharp, and capable of being recalled and injected when the loop is trying to run. Long, poetic affirmations fail here. The mind can't access them when under threat. Your code must cut through noise like a blade.

Injection in Action

Let's say you're in a moment where your default loop wants to run. The trigger is active. Maybe someone just ignored your message. Maybe you walked into a room and felt invisible. The mind starts pulling the old file: "You don't matter," or "They always overlook you." This is the moment the injection must enter.

Pause.

Feel the instinct to spiral.

Interrupt it — not with analysis, not with negotiation — but with the command.

Say it internally like you're giving an order, not a wish.

"I create my signal. I don't wait to be picked."

Hold it for a few seconds. Not as hope, but as directive.

You'll feel the loop trying to reassert itself. Let it pass like background noise. You're not arguing with it. You're not suppressing it. You're simply not running that file anymore.

Even if the emotion doesn't fully shift, something deeper starts listening. The command isn't for your surface thoughts. It's for the code behind them. Repeat the command silently or out loud as needed, especially while you hold the energy of the new response. Move differently. Sit differently. Take one action that aligns with the new instruction. This anchors it. Now it's not just code — it's embodied.

The real power of code injection is not in the words themselves but in your decision to become the one issuing commands instead of following inherited ones. This shift — from being the system to becoming the programmer — is the pivot point of transformation.

You're not trying to fix yourself. You're not rehearsing positivity. You are speaking into the system and watching it obey. This is not bypass. This is reprogramming.

It will feel unfamiliar at first. The mind will doubt it. The body might hesitate. That's not failure. That's confirmation you've stepped outside the loop.

Hold the command anyway.

This is how reality begins to reorganize around new architecture. Not by hoping it will. Not by waiting to feel different. But by issuing clean code and holding your field long enough for the system to obey.

The more you inject with clarity, the less the old scripts will find space to run. And in time, the default itself rewrites. You are no longer the product of loops. You're the one injecting the pattern. You're the architect now.

Anchoring the Rewrite: Making It Stick in the Physical

You can script a new command. You can interrupt an old loop. But if that rewrite stays only in your mind, it tends to fade. Your nervous system still remembers how it used to respond. Your posture, your tone, your habits still echo the old identity. This is why even the most powerful breakthroughs sometimes feel like they vanish a day later. There was no anchor. There was no physical lock-in.

To reprogram your system fully, the rewrite needs a place to live. Not just in thought, but in form. In how you breathe, how you move, how you dress, how you speak. Otherwise, the rewrite stays theoretical. Anchoring makes it real. It gives the new command a rhythm, a place, and a home in your body.

Anchoring is not about adding more rituals for the sake of it. It's about installing the new command into the physical layer where your past scripts used to dominate. When your body starts to expect the new pattern and react as if it's normal, that's when the rewrite truly sticks.

The Importance of Repetition Without Reverting

If you've ever had a moment of insight followed by a sense of failure when you "fell back" into old patterns, it's usually not because you lost the insight. It's because the new signal hadn't yet taken root in the physical. You were mentally convinced, but physically unanchored. The nervous system doesn't learn through epiphany. It learns through repetition. Not the shallow kind where you mindlessly repeat a phrase, but embodied repetition, where every gesture, choice, and micro-movement begins to align with the new script.

This is what makes a rewrite permanent. Not perfection, but consistency. And consistency is built from ritual — a deliberate series of actions that signal to your system, "this is what we run now."

Anchoring isn't about being spiritual. It's about being programmable. And your body is programmable through physical cues, not just internal beliefs.

Anchoring Ritual: Physicalizing the New Identity

Let's create an anchoring ritual that allows you to install a new command at the body level. Choose a rewrite you've already created — something you want to hold and live from. Now we're going to assign it a *physical anchor point* in your day. This must be something real, repeatable, and sensory. The more it engages your body, the deeper the installation.

For example, let's say your rewrite is: *"I move as if I belong."*

Pick a physical act you do every morning — brushing your teeth, showering, putting on your shoes. You're going to overlay the command onto this moment, not as a thought, but as an energy you act from.

Let's say you pick putting on your shoes. For the next seven days, every time you do it, you do it deliberately, with the energy of your rewrite fully embodied. You feel the ground under you as territory you claim. You tie the laces not as someone preparing to "go out" but as someone stepping into their space. You walk from that moment as if the rewrite had already completed.

No explanations. No trying to "feel" the belief. Just act as if the new signal already defines you. That's anchoring. The mind may resist at first. The emotions may lag behind. But the body moves. And that movement speaks louder than belief.

We'll now take this anchoring further and make it flexible, so it integrates with more moments across your day, not just one. This is where the rewrite begins to override the default without needing your constant attention.

To deepen the anchor, you must allow it to ripple through more layers of your day. One moment is a seed, but multiple physical entry points create a field. This doesn't mean you force the rewrite at every turn. It means you weave it in where friction is lowest. You choose familiar moments and overlay the new signal.

Look for rhythms. Anything you do daily can become an anchor point. When you reach for the door handle before leaving home. When you open your laptop. When you make your morning beverage. These are not just habits. They're portals. You can layer your new command onto these actions by adding subtle embodiment: a breath, a shift in posture, a glance upward, a whispered line, a single second of presence. The goal is not to "believe harder," but to *install more often*.

What this builds is muscle memory. Not just muscular in the body, but muscular in the energy field. Your system begins to recognize this identity as default. The more often you behave as this version of you, even without proof, the more natural it becomes to stay in that pattern.

You will know the anchor has taken when you catch yourself mid-action and realize you're already living the rewrite. Without trying. Without pushing. Just moving from it. That's when it becomes less of a practice and more of a presence.

Now take it even further. Create a *closing ritual*. Most people think rewrites happen only in the activation phase. But the nervous system also learns through how you close. How you end your day. How you unplug. How you process what didn't match. A closing ritual tells the system: *we are still in the new pattern, even when things feel incomplete.*

This doesn't have to be dramatic. Even standing in front of a mirror for five seconds before bed, holding eye contact with yourself, and nodding once is enough. You're affirming the code: *We ran it today. We'll run it again.* No shame. No correction. Just anchoring.

This is what removes the loop of failure. Instead of asking "Did I stay in the new energy all day?" you ask, "Did I return to it? Did I install it at least once with precision?" That's what matters. Rewrites stick through repetition, not perfection. The ego wants spectacle. The system wants reliability.

Finally, claim a phrase that seals the anchor. Not an affirmation. A command. Something short and sharp. Three to five words. You speak it only when the signal is strong, so the nervous system links it to power. Over time, that phrase becomes a neural shortcut. Just saying it evokes the rewrite state.

Use this phrase sparingly. Not out of habit, but as ignition. Think of it as a physical button that drops you back into the new pattern. The command becomes both cue and confirmation. You're not repeating it to convince yourself. You're confirming what's already true in the field.

Anchoring is not maintenance. It is integration. It takes the ephemeral and gives it bones. It closes the gap between thought and reality by embedding new code in movement, presence, and repetition.

The rewrite was never meant to stay in the mind. It belongs in your breath, your spine, your steps, and the smallest rituals that define your day. When it lives there, it no longer needs to be remembered. It becomes who you are.

Chapter 12. Exit the Game, Enter the Code

The Final Detachment: Leaving the System Without Running Away

There's a point on the path where the desire to detach becomes overwhelming. The noise, the manipulation, the relentless cycles can feel so synthetic, so hollow, that you begin to crave escape. You want to disappear, to unplug, to sever all ties with the matrix of roles, rules, and repetition. This instinct is not wrong. It's a sign you've seen the script for what it is. But detachment isn't disappearance. And escape isn't freedom.

Leaving the system isn't about vanishing from the world. It's about exiting the agreement. The system only holds power over those who still play by its terms. These terms are mostly invisible: prove your worth, chase the next level, earn rest, obey authority, suppress discomfort, fear stillness. They're built into language, institutions, even your own inner dialogue. And most of them aren't enforced externally. You enforce them yourself, out of habit and programming.

The final detachment begins when you stop reacting to those terms. You no longer rise to meet them. You stop proving, defending, or seeking validation from those who never had your blueprint in their hands. You become invisible to the control grid, not by hiding, but by ceasing to feed it your energy. You learn to walk through it untouched. Not because you escaped, but because you no longer speak its language.

This form of detachment is quiet. It doesn't require rebellion or dramatic exits. You might still go to the same job. Still speak to the same people. Still use the same tools. But the script is no longer active in you. You're not in resistance, which is still a form of engagement. You're in neutrality, which is pure sovereignty.

You begin to choose what aligns with your frequency, not what earns you approval. You feel what's true for you without needing permission to act on it. You stop seeking external confirmation before moving forward. And most importantly, you stop waiting for the system to change before you let yourself live.

This is a powerful shift because it removes dependency. Many people believe they must first fix the external world before they can be free. They spend years trying to reform institutions, wake others up, or dismantle oppressive narratives. While this work has value, it can become another trap. If your liberation is conditional on collective change, you are still bound. Real detachment means no longer needing the system to collapse in order for you to rise.

Of course, there will still be friction. Bills may still arrive. People may still misunderstand you. The structures of the world may still demand attention. But you're no longer negotiating with them from a place of fear. You engage only when necessary, and even then, you do it on your terms. Not because you're trying to win, but because you've already left. What they offer can no longer define you.

There's a subtle power in this form of presence. It radiates calm authority. You're not trying to convert anyone. You're not trying to win an argument. You've simply stopped participating in the game that says you need to earn your existence. The world will still see you. But it won't know how to pull you back in. You've become ungraspable.

You'll start to notice that the more you stop feeding the system with your attention, the less it tries to control you. The hooks weaken. The provocations lose their grip. People who once mirrored your old loops begin to fade into the background. Situations that used to pull you into conflict or confusion pass by like harmless static. This isn't because the world has become softer. It's because your field is no longer tuned to those frequencies.

This is what detachment truly creates: a new frequency landscape. And in that landscape, reality begins to restructure itself around your non-reaction. Not as passivity, but as mastery. You no longer operate from urgency. You begin to trust the delay, the pause, the space before action. You're not rushed into proving you're right or defending your new identity. Silence becomes your ally. Stillness becomes a declaration.

This level of clarity cannot be faked. You can't pretend to be detached while secretly hoping others will notice your glow. You can't detach halfway while still needing applause for your healing. You either let go of the contract, or you don't. And when you do, the peace that follows doesn't feel like a reward. It feels like remembering. Like returning to a version of yourself that was never seeking, never performing, never surviving.

The irony is that you become more present, not less. You show up more fully, not because you're trying to prove something, but because there's no more internal resistance. You begin to experience the world from a place of openness, not fear. You move through relationships without needing to control how others see you. You create without needing to predict how it will be received. You walk without armor because nothing outside you determines your safety.

There will still be moments when the old pull returns. A situation might tempt you to prove your worth. An interaction might invite you back into an outdated identity. These are not failures. They are opportunities to choose again. To remember what you've exited. You can feel the pull without answering it. That is the rewiring. That is the detachment being reinforced in real time.

You may notice you lose interest in certain conversations. You may no longer have the urge to correct misconceptions or defend your path. You conserve your energy not as a strategy, but as a natural result of no longer leaking power into illusions. This is when you start to realize that most of the "fights" you thought you had to win were optional. Most of the structures you feared were illusions held in place by your attention.

This is not abandonment of responsibility. In fact, your sense of responsibility deepens. But it shifts direction. Instead of being responsible for upholding the expectations of the world, you become responsible for staying aligned with your internal signal. You answer to that signal. You calibrate to it. That is your new authority.

And with that comes the ultimate paradox: when you no longer need to escape, you're free. When you no longer fear being seen or misunderstood, you become invisible in the most powerful way. Not hidden, but untouchable. Not withdrawn, but sovereign. You've left the system, not by running away, but by refusing to run at all.

The door was never locked. You just had to stop asking for permission to walk through it.

Script Autonomy: How to Program a Life That Obeys Only You

Autonomy is not about living off-grid or rejecting society. It's not rebellion for the sake of rebellion. True script autonomy is about internal authorship. It's the shift from being a character reacting inside a story you didn't write, to becoming the one who chooses the structure, the tone, and the direction of that story. You stop outsourcing your decisions to invisible scripts. You stop letting others' programs run your life. You become the sole operator of your personal system.

Most people live according to inherited scripts. These scripts are absorbed early, encoded through repetition, social pressure, emotional trauma, and survival adaptation. "Be nice to be loved." "Work hard to earn worth." "Don't outshine others." "Follow the path to stay safe." These are not truths. They're behavioral algorithms dressed up as virtues. And unless challenged, they run in the background, guiding everything from who you date to how you think about money or health.

The first layer of script autonomy requires brutal clarity. You must detect which scripts are still active and ask: do they serve your direction, or do they bind it? This is not about blaming the source of the script. It doesn't matter if it came from school, parents, religion, or culture. What matters is whether it still has a grip on your decisions. If it does, it's active code.

You don't dismantle these codes by arguing with them. You replace them with your own. This is where most people get stuck. They try to use logic to unlearn emotional patterns. But emotional patterns were not created through logic. They were created through repeated sensory, relational, and energetic experiences. So the rewrite must follow that same language. You must build new scripts not only with thought, but with action, embodiment, and environment.

To create a life that obeys only you, you must learn to think like a programmer of reality. That means mapping your own logic, assigning value only where you choose to, and designing input systems that automatically return the output you want. This is not metaphysical theory. It is a structure for conscious living. Your inner code becomes the blueprint that life reflects back.

Let's take a practical example. If your inherited script says, "Discomfort means something is wrong," your system will constantly flag growth as danger. You will retreat from newness. You will overthink every risk. That script doesn't care about your dreams. It only cares about preserving its loop. But if you rewrite the code to, "Discomfort means I'm expanding capacity," your body will begin to respond differently to challenge. The same situation triggers a different physiological and emotional response, because the script running the interpretation has changed.

This isn't a one-time shift. It's a process of full-spectrum programming. Thoughts, words, micro-decisions, tone of voice, posture, and personal environment must all align with the new script. This is how you anchor autonomy in the physical. You're not just thinking new thoughts. You're building a system around them. A system that does not default back to the old loop just because you're tired, stressed, or uncertain.

Most people live inside permission-based frameworks. They act when others validate their path. They speak when it's safe. They move when they're sure they'll succeed. But that model produces delayed sovereignty. You become autonomous only after the world approves your shift. And by then, it's not autonomy anymore. It's just a response to a green light that wasn't yours to give.

True script autonomy begins when you remove that external gate. When you create, act, and move based on the clarity of your own internal protocol. The moment you start living that way, your nervous system might panic. It's not used to operating without outer checkpoints. It will try to reach for feedback, reassurance, or cues from others. This is where the second half of your programming process begins.

It will feel like flying without instruments. You'll be tempted to copy from someone else's map, to borrow language or behavior that seems to work for them. But autonomy cannot be inherited. It must be built in real time, from your own signal. That signal doesn't come from certainty. It comes from resonance. You begin to detect what strengthens your energy, what pulls you into coherence, what decisions make your system feel like it's clicking into place.

This is where most people fall into the trap of spiritual mimicry. They wear autonomy like a costume, adopting confident behaviors, repeating empowered mantras, but still relying on external scaffolding. They haven't collapsed the deeper dependency structure. True autonomy only begins when you can function clearly without mirroring anyone else's values, pace, preferences, or priorities. That means letting go of the need to be understood or applauded for your choices. Not because you're cold, but because you're tuned into a deeper feedback system—your own.

Your nervous system may resist this shift, especially if it's spent a lifetime in approval-based operating modes. That's why autonomy is not a mindset but a rewiring. You must repattern your system's response to silence, disapproval, uncertainty, and solitude. You teach your body that being misread or judged is not a threat. You show it, repeatedly, that safety comes from alignment, not from belonging to a group script.

To embody this, create a daily feedback loop that doesn't rely on external results. The way to maintain autonomy without drifting is to design your own internal scorecard. Choose a small set of behaviors that reflect your chosen script, and track only those. Not outcomes. Not opinions. Not rewards. If your script says "I lead with clarity," then clarity in your speech, posture, and decision-making becomes your metric—not whether someone agreed with your choice. This makes your process self-sustaining.

You'll begin to notice that old patterns try to sneak back in through energetic backdoors—through relationships, routines, and even internal thoughts that seem innocent. For example, you might still find yourself explaining your decisions to people who didn't ask. That's an echo of the old script needing permission to exist. Or you might dress a bold move in soft language to seem less threatening. That's your system asking to be liked before it fully detaches.

To seal the new script, you need to treat every moment of autonomy as a rite. Not a performance, but a practice of alignment. Every time you speak truth without decoration, every time you move without justifying, every time you say no without guilt, you are strengthening the system. These are not small acts. They are code injections. The program is learning to run a different OS.

Eventually, reality begins to match your new architecture. Not because you forced it, but because your field now emits a coherent signature. You no longer vibrate in and out of identity depending on context. You're not performing one version of self for work, another for intimacy, and another for solitude. You are unified. That unity is not rigid, but clear. It doesn't mean you stop evolving. It means your evolution is self-directed.

In this space, you begin to experience a kind of quiet power. You're no longer trying to dominate reality or bend it into shape. You're not chasing autonomy through rebellion or detachment. You're simply operating from your own script, which was always the point. You are not a reaction to the system. You are the system. And that shift, once made, cannot be undone. Autonomy becomes your natural frequency. You no longer ask for alignment. You generate it. You no longer hope for resonance. You become the source. The life you program now is not one that follows you—it's one that obeys because it recognizes who wrote it.

The Return: Walking as the Programmer in a World of Players

There comes a moment when the inner work stops feeling like work. It becomes motion. Rhythm. A silent frequency that pulses beneath every step you take. This is the return. Not a retreat into who you were, but a reentry into the world with a different internal structure. You no longer see yourself as a seeker trying to learn how the system works. You've built your own. You're walking as the one who writes the code.

And yet, the world remains filled with players. People still running on borrowed scripts, default settings, emotional triggers that echo through crowds. It can be tempting to separate from them, to feel above the noise, or to isolate entirely. But walking as the programmer doesn't mean escaping the game. It means moving through it with sovereign authorship. You are not trying to wake everyone up. You are simply not sleeping anymore.

In this state, you begin to notice the quiet spaces where reality bends more easily. Conversations shift when you enter a room. Timelines feel pliable. Responses don't feel random anymore. You see them as outputs, reactions to a field that you've consciously set. This is not about superiority. It's about responsibility. Your very presence becomes instructional. Without trying to convince, explain, or correct, you begin to carry signal. People feel it before they understand it.

But with this shift comes a subtle test: can you stay seated in this identity when others don't recognize it? Can you remain the author when the world still relates to the character you used to play? That moment when someone speaks to you like the old version of yourself—that's your prompt. That's the test of embodiment. Do you answer as the player? Or as the one who designed the role?

This is where embodiment becomes more than emotional alignment. It becomes behavioral precision. You don't just feel different. You speak, move, and decide from the new code. Not out of habit. Out of command. That's what walking as the programmer looks like in the world of players. You are not adjusting yourself to their loops. You're maintaining your own. To practice this, pay attention to micro-moments where your old identity would have reacted. A small irritation, a need to justify, a hunger to be validated. These are not failures. They're signals. They show you exactly where a little residue of the old programming still runs in the background. Don't fight it. Observe it like code. Read the pattern. Then inject the new command—not to suppress, but to reroute.

For example, if someone dismisses your idea in a meeting, and your body tenses with the urge to defend, notice the old script. It may say, "If I don't speak up now, I'll be disrespected." Pause. Breathe. Ask: What would the programmer do? Maybe it's speaking calmly with full authority. Maybe it's letting the moment pass because you've already calibrated the field. Maybe it's something entirely unexpected. What matters is that it comes from alignment, not from the loop.

This is not passive. It's precise. And it takes energy. But not the kind of energy that burns out. The more you walk this way, the more your field stabilizes. The more you resist falling into reaction, the more reality begins to reconfigure around your steadiness. People either adapt or fall away. Opportunities recalibrate. Timelines rearrange. Not because you pushed—but because you held.

That steadiness is not rigidity. It's not cold detachment or indifference. It's the absence of performance. You are no longer trying to become. You are being. This is what people feel but can't name. They sense that you're not looking to be liked, followed, or understood. You're not unconsciously adjusting your energy to avoid rejection or secure approval. You are broadcasting something deeper. Something that rewrites the room.

When you walk this way, your presence becomes polarizing. Not because you're loud, but because you're clear. Some will feel inspired and want to shift with you. Others may feel exposed. Not by anything you say, but by what you no longer validate. The more you embody the script you've chosen, the less you echo the collective distortions. And the less you echo, the more visible those distortions become. To some, you will feel like permission. To others, a threat.

This is not personal. It's code in motion. The programmer does not apologize for having rewritten the script. But they also don't seek to dominate with it. Your energy is not a weapon. It's a current. And the cleaner you run it, the more it calls into form what is resonant and dissolves what is not.

There will still be moments where the old reality tugs at you. Where someone tries to pull you into a dynamic that no longer fits. Where an environment attempts to make you forget the access you've earned. These are not setbacks. They are checkpoints. Opportunities to breathe, to pause, to remember. Embodiment is not a final state. It's a maintained frequency. And each moment you hold it deepens the script. Locks it in.

This is also the space where silent rituals matter most. Not grand declarations or daily affirmations shouted into a mirror. But quiet calibrations. Tiny, sacred checks where you realign yourself before the external world catches your attention. Ask yourself: Who am I walking as today? What field am I broadcasting? Is my behavior matching my blueprint?

You begin to notice the difference between force and presence. Between trying to influence a room and simply holding a frequency that rearranges it. Between saying something to convince and saying it because it's true. There is no longer a need to prove your shift. It expresses itself. In the way you move. In the pauses you allow. In the silence you hold without anxiety. That is the real mark of transformation.

To sustain this, you must build inner infrastructure. Not control mechanisms, but energetic architecture. Practices that keep you tuned even when the world gets noisy. Walks without headphones. Conscious stillness in public spaces. Intentional breath before speaking. Micro-actions that remind your system: I am not a participant. I am the one setting the frequency.

You'll start to recognize others walking this path. Not because they use the same words, but because their presence feels untangled. There is no hook, no pull, no hidden ask in their energy. Just signal. This is how programmers identify one another. Not through talk, but through texture.

And if the world tries to pull you back into the old loop, remember this: you don't have to leave the field to remain sovereign within it. Your autonomy is not built on withdrawal. It's built on clarity. You are not trying to escape the system. You are walking through it like it obeys you. Because it does. Not in theory. In lived, embodied reality.

That's what it means to walk as the programmer. You're no longer a product of the code. You are its author. And you've stopped writing loops. You've started building exits.

www.ingramcontent.com/pod-product-compliance
Lightning Source LLC
Chambersburg PA
CBHW072140160426
43197CB00012B/2188